THE SLEEPING BEAUTIES

by Robert Alan Evans

‖SAMUEL FRENCH‖

samuelfrench.co.uk

Copyright © 2013 Robert Alan Evans
2016 by Robert Alan Evans
All Rights Reserved

THE SLEEPING BEAUTIES, is fully protected under the copyright laws of the British Commonwealth, including Canada, the United States of America, and all other countries of the Copyright Union. All rights, including professional and amateur stage productions, recitation, lecturing, public reading, motion picture, radio broadcasting, television and the rights of translation into foreign languages are strictly reserved.

ISBN 978-0-573-11194-5

www.samuelfrench.co.uk

www.samuelfrench.com

FOR AMATEUR PRODUCTION ENQUIRIES

UNITED KINGDOM AND WORLD
EXCLUDING NORTH AMERICA
plays@SamuelFrench-London.co.uk
020 7255 4302/01
Each title is subject to availability from Samuel French,
depending upon country of performance.

CAUTION: Professional and amateur producers are hereby warned that *THE SLEEPING BEAUTIES* is subject to a licensing fee. Publication of this play does not imply availability for performance. Both amateurs and professionals considering a production are strongly advised to apply to the appropriate agent before starting rehearsals, advertising or booking a theatre. A licensing fee must be paid whether the title is presented for charity or gain and whether or not admission is charged.

The professional rights in this play are controlled by Casarotto Ramsay Associates, Waverley House, 7-12 Noel Street, London, W1F 8GQ

No one shall make any changes in this title for the purpose of production. No part of this book may be reproduced, stored in a retrieval system, or transmitted in any form, by any means, now known or yet to be invented, including mechanical, electronic, photocopying, recording, videotaping, or otherwise, without the prior written permission of the publisher. No one shall upload this title, or part of this title, to any social media websites.

The right of Robert Alan Evans to be identified as author of this work has been asserted in accordance with Section 77 of the Copyright, Designs and Patents Act 1988.

First performed by Sherman Cymru on 11th December 2013

Author's Note

When I think of fairy tales it's usually a jumble in my head; a pair of red shoes, a frog or two, a little pig, an evil stepmother, a house made of sweets, a wolf, sharp teeth, some pebbles in the moonlight, forests and forests and forests, the crying of a baby, a world frozen, a billy-goat bleating, turkish delight, flying through the night, a flash of red amongst the trees. But through all of it runs something dark, something terrifying, the thing that keeps us going back for more. I think it is this darkness that keeps a fairy tale alive. It is what we start wanting when we are little; to be scared, to imagine ourselves lost in the woods, to think what we would do when the wolf came to our door or the witch started to cackle.

These stories aren't suitable for children, which is what makes them so irresistible. Hack off her toe, pluck out his eyes, starve her, beat him, pull her hair out, kill his parents, leave them in the woods, let the bears eat them, lock them in a cage, burn them, burn them, BURN THEM!

We need to feel terror, we need to care, we need to see that some little children go wrong. Why else would Roald Dahl be so popular? And so it is with fairy tales. Whatever we do we mustn't make them feel safe. And I think that this is as true today as it ever was.

Once upon a time a child would go off the path, probably see something unexpected and then get eaten, the end. Don't go off the path! Then, somewhere along the way the girls in these stories seemed to lose the ability to fight, run or even, on occasion, speak. Their words were the words of their elders, their fathers or the prince that would save them. To me this is as great a danger as anything you might find in a forest at night or in winter. It is the danger of being told you must fit into a certain story and it crosses over from fiction into real life all too easily.

My friend told me that at parties her young boys are always being asked 'What are you doing at the moment? Are you going to go and climb that or run over there?' Whereas to girls it's often 'You look lovely. You look so pretty. Your dress is lovely.' I think this is why we need our fairy tales to be dangerous. They need to challenge. They need to tell people that there are a million different stories and probably one of them will be about someone like you. Boys are not always action and girls are not always appearance. You don't have to get married to a prince, or even married. You might not always be happy ever after, but you can understand, you can know the world and see how it creates and controls your narrative.

And so to *The Sleeping Beauties*. I hope it is funny. I hope it still feels like a fairy tale. I hope, on occasion, it is scary. And I hope that if I were, say, ten-years-old again, with all the worries and insecurities a ten-year-old has to deal with, I would think it was for me.

Robert Alan Evans
2016

ACT I

SCENE ONE Once Upon A Time
SCENE TWO A Promise Made, A Friend Saved
SCENE THREE The Queen Lies
SCENE FOUR The Pregnancy And Birth
SCENE FIVE The Naming Ceremony
SCENE SIX Rose Is Executed And The Girls Grow Up
SCENE SEVEN Preparing For The 15th Birthday Party
SCENE EIGHT The Dress Fitting
SCENE NINE The 15th Birthday Party
SCENE TEN A Pact To Run Away
SCENE ELEVEN Eve Discovers The Curse
SCENE TWELVE The Spinning Wheel
SCENE THIRTEEN Time Passes And The Prince Arrives
Interval

ACT II

SCENE ONE Time Has Passed
SCENE TWO The Glowworms
SCENE THREE Queenie Meets Dawn And Eve
SCENE FOUR The Palace And The Facemakers
SCENE FIVE Echo
SCENE SIX Getting Ready For The Pig Ball
SCENE SEVEN The Pig Ball
SCENE EIGHT Eve Finds Echo And A Spell Is Cast
SCENE NINE A Near Kiss And A Fight
SCENE TEN Eve Goes Into The Wilderness
SCENE ELEVEN Cold Feet
SCENE TWELVE The Stories Untold
SCENE THIRTEEN The Wedding Ceremony
Epilogue

To Mum and Dad
Who help me always

CHARACTERS

ROSE/EVE
QUEEN/DAWN
CLOVE/QUEENIE
FERTILITY WIFE/PAVLOVA/ECHO
PRINCE
MAXI/BONE/SANDÉ
KING/MINI/POKE/JOILÉ

ACT I

Scene One
Once Upon A Time

An old woman is sitting as the audience comes in. She is playing a strange tune on the harmonica. She is magic. She is the forest. She watches us come in and sit. Then, when we are sat down…

FERTILITY WIFE Old.

I'm old, aren't I?

Just an old woman.

But you know, when I close my eyes there's so much more.

It's how I remember nowadays.

Yes.

She closes her eyes. A sound starts to swell.

Once…

Once upon a time there was a great forest.

Hear it.

Hear it as it once more creeps across the land.

A forest so great it covered almost all the earth.

A forest once, was where I lived.

Me and my kind.

Those who had magic.

Great forces lay in the forest.

Forces that were older than 'good' or 'bad'.

And respect them, we did. Learned to use their magic.

Except for one. One who went bad. A great talent he had for magic, but he went too far, thought he could control a darker force and was struck down, thrown from the forest.

And so he schemed and plotted. Bided his time.

Until one day...

A king came to the throne.

A king who had just one flaw. His pride. He could never admit to being wrong.

And through this little flaw the wicked one entered.

Flattering and fawning he worked his way to the king.

And when the queen failed to conceive the blame was put on the forest and us that lived there.

The **KING** *gets up to speak. A bombastic speech. We just see his face lit high up on stage. His voice echoes across the land.* **CLOVE** *is controlling every word he says.*

CLOVE I have been informed...

KING I have been informed (**CLOVE**'s *voice runs under the* **KING**'s *then trails off*) that some of those that live in the forest, the so called 'Fertility Wives' are trying to undermine our power. That they try and threaten this kingdom.

Well hear this!

From now on the forest and the witches who live there are branded enemies of the kingdom.

They will be hanged.

All visits to the forest will cease immediately and work will begin on the great wall that will protect us.

CLOVE *whispers.*

Furthermore, there shall be no more babies, no more pregnancies, until my wife is with child.

No one shall have a baby before the King.

On pain of death!

The **KING** *collapses.* **CLOVE** *strokes him.*

FERTILITY WIFE And so it was the great war started between those who loved beauty and those who would destroy it.

The **FERTILITY WIFE** *plays a screeching note on her harmonica and disappears. The note left to resonate. A scream in the forest at night.*

***

Scene Two
A Promise Made, A Friend Saved

The forest. Dark. A storm. The **QUEEN** *and* **ROSE** *appear. They are cold and wet and struggling. They hear the scream.*

QUEEN What was that?

She calms herself. Notices that **ROSE** *isn't next to her.*

ROSE *has stopped and is holding her belly.*

Rose, what's wrong?

ROSE Nothing. Nothing. I'm fine.

There is a lightning flash and again we hear the scream in the night, closer now. The sound of something getting closer. Breathing. Hunting. The slavering of an animal. The sound has something in common with **CLOVE**. **ROSE** *and the* **QUEEN** *are back to back.*

QUEEN Who's there?

I said who's there?

The sound gets closer. Terrifying.

Suddenly there is a blinding flash.

The screech of an animal that has been wounded. A yelp as it moves off.

Then something appears, a shadow.

The storm calms.

An old woman steps into the light.

She has her helpers **MAXI** *and* **MINI** *with her.*

FERTILITY WIFE Late.

Bit late. Don't you think?

Want to watch out.

QUEEN Who are you?

FERTILITY WIFE I'm an old woman, see. Mushroom picking.

MINI *laughs.*

Sorry if we... frightened you.

QUEEN Do you live here?

FERTILITY WIFE Oh yes.

Got an old gingerbread house in the woods.

Only joking.

MAXI *laughs a bit gormlessly.*

(spotting a mushroom) Ooooh there. Maxi!

MAXI *gets the mushroom and brings it back.*

QUEEN I came to find the witches who live here.

MINI Witches?!

QUEEN The Wives. Do you know them?

FERTILITY WIFE Might do.

QUEEN You have to take me to them. Please.

FERTILITY WIFE 'Take'? 'Have to'? I don't think so my dear.

ROSE We should get back, your –

QUEEN Rose!

FERTILITY WIFE Your what?

QUEEN We need to find the Fertility Wives. We need their help.

FERTILITY WIFE With what?

QUEEN My friend...she's pregnant.

FERTILITY WIFE Then she'll die.

QUEEN No.

FERTILITY WIFE Yes yes yes.

Head chopped off.

Hung from a tree.

The king says so and so shall it be.

Holding out the mushroom again.

You sure you won't have a bit?

ROSE has pain in her belly again. She crumples over.

QUEEN Rose. Rose.

Are you okay?

What's wrong?

The woman watches as the QUEEN holds ROSE.

She looks up and we hear an incantation in the air again.

ROSE's pain eases.

The woman kneels down and looks at ROSE.

ROSE sees her through the pain.

ROSE Is the baby okay?

FERTILITY WIFE Yes.

ROSE's pain passes.

The child is safe.

ROSE smiles.

QUEEN How did you do that?

FERTILITY WIFE I should not…

Sad times are here. You know that?

ROSE nods.

The child can pass.

If you want.

ROSE I can't.

FERTILITY WIFE Then die you will.

QUEEN You're one of them.

FERTILITY WIFE A witch? Isn't that what your husband likes to call us? Your highness.

QUEEN You have to help us.

FERTILITY WIFE No.

I know what you want.

A baby.

A baby to save your friend.

A baby to tell your husband.

Oh the king will be pleased.

A baby at last.

But no.

QUEEN Please.

FERTILITY WIFE Do you know what he's done, your husband?

He has let evil into the kingdom.

Building this wall.

Killed off all my kind.

Until there's just me left.

An old woman. Left to bury her sisters.

Your husband… I hate your husband. I hate him.

QUEEN He thinks the witches want to destroy the kingdom. Kill his people.

FERTILITY WIFE He is a fool. We are forbidden from killing.

QUEEN Then help me. If he could see a child on the way he'd change. He's a good man.

FERTILITY WIFE turns away.

QUEEN Then you've broken your promise.

FERTILITY WIFE What?

QUEEN You said you're forbidden from killing. But you won't help.

FERTILITY WIFE No.

QUEEN Then you're killing any woman who falls pregnant.

FERTILITY WIFE …

QUEEN Give me a child. Let me change him.

FERTILITY WIFE You would swear an oath on it?

ROSE Your majesty…

QUEEN Shhhh

> *Looking at* **ROSE**.
>
> I have to save you.
>
> *(to* **FERTILITY WIFE***)* Yes.

FERTILITY WIFE On the child's life?

> *The* **QUEEN** *nods*.
>
> Not just a nod. A nod won't do.
>
> You swear on the child's life that you will stop the king.
>
> Stop him building the wall. Let the forest breathe once more.

QUEEN If you give me a child, I swear on its life that the king will leave you and the forest alone.

FERTILITY WIFE A child is a thing of love.

> You must love.

QUEEN I do love.

> I love Rose.

FERTILITY WIFE Yes.

> And the two of you must be bound together.
>
> *To* **ROSE**.
>
> Do you agree?
>
> **ROSE** *nods*.
>
> Then know this.
>
> *Incantations happen.*
>
> The world is older than you or I.
>
> The dark has light the light will die.
>
> And time will pass in the blink of an eye.
>
> A promise made cannot be undone.
>
> A promise made on not just one
>
> But two lives.

Two lives lying in wait.

Still dreaming.

Feel them gathering.

You feel?

Two lives I weave together.

The **FERTILITY WIFE** *feels something strange. Something is not right with the* **QUEEN**.

Someone has put a spell on you.

Dark magic.

A spell that would have stopped you ever falling pregnant.

The **FERTILITY WIFE** *concentrates.*

Forest deep I call on you. Darkness I call on you. The spirits who have lived here for all memory I call on you.

Throw this out.

Throw this out.

You who cannot stand beauty.

I say to you 'BEGONE'

BEGONE!

The **QUEEN** *jolts. A scream is heard fading away into the night.*

Strong. He gets stronger.

QUEEN Who?

FERTILITY WIFE The one who hates all beauty. Wishes only to destroy it.

You know him when you see him. A pity your husband does not.

You two must not fail me.

You understand?

All our futures depend on it.

QUEEN We won't.

I just. I need a child.

FERTILITY WIFE Done. Dusted.

Can't you feel it?

Done.

I've done my part. Now you must keep your promise.

QUEEN Yes.

FERTILITY WIFE Keep your promise or you'll feel the darker side of the forest.

The **FERTILITY WIFE** *disappears.*

***

Scene Three
The Queen Lies

*The **KING** is with **CLOVE**. **CLOVE** is trying to get him to sign a document.*

CLOVE We need more workers your highness. The wall is nearly complete. It just needs one last push.

KING We don't have any more men. Everyone is already working double time.

CLOVE Men, no. But there are certain jobs that could be done just as well by a child.

KING You want the children working on this?

CLOVE Only those from the outlying villages. The ones from the poorer homes. They could help support their families.

KING I'm not sure.

CLOVE It is their future they would be protecting. Only say… all those over the age of five.

KING Five?

CLOVE Four then.

Beat.

Why not your gracefullness? They could collect stones, mix the mortar. It's not like they'd be doing anything else.

KING What about their schooling?

CLOVE Sire. Do these children really need school? It's not like they're going to amount to much. School should be preserved for the more prosperous families. It's wasted on the poor.

KING But my father…

CLOVE Your father lived in a different age. The king could afford to be generous. Things have changed. Our enemies in the forest grow stronger. We need to protect ourselves. I've drawn up a document, it just needs your signature.

KING I'm not sure.

> CLOVE *gets impatient and we see the kings eyes glaze over.*

CLOVE You will build this wall.

KING *(repeating)* I will build this wall.

CLOVE Whatever it takes.

KING Whatever it takes.

CLOVE Now sign the document.

KING I will sign…

> *The* KING *goes to sign, but the* QUEEN *comes in before he can and the spell is broken.* CLOVE *is annoyed.*

QUEEN What's going on here then darling? All this muttering.

CLOVE The king is undertaking serious business.

QUEEN What business?

CLOVE It's really not…

QUEEN I wasn't talking to you.

KING *(confused)* Darling I was… I believe I was…

> *The* QUEEN *takes the document and reads it quickly.*

QUEEN I presume you're not going to sign this.

KING Well…

> *The* QUEEN *rips up the document, to* CLOVE*'s horror.*

CLOVE Your majesty you –

QUEEN *(ignoring* CLOVE*)* Children? Working? Your father would never have allowed it. And neither will you.

KING Darling the wall –

QUEEN I'm sick of it. This whole wall business.

Have you forgotten how we used to meet together in the forest?

KING *(smiling)* Of course not.

QUEEN That wasn't strictly 'allowed' was it?

KING Your father would've blown his top if he'd known.

QUEEN Lovers. Lovers in the woods. It's happened forever, don't you think?

CLOVE Changed times your highness. The threat to our whole way of life –

KING I loved you from the very first moment I saw you.

QUEEN Then stop building this wall. Let others meet, like we did. Let them love.

We *need* the forest. Your people have connections to it.

CLOVE Like your maid?

Rose, isn't it?

ROSE, *who has been standing in the corner, tries to make herself invisible.*

Yes.

Your family came from the forest, didn't they?

QUEEN Leave her alone.

CLOVE But your highness. As chief physician and advisor I have responsibility for your health and that of all the women in the royal household and I must say Rose is looking a bit pale.

Yes.

Definitely.

Are you okay, Rose?

ROSE *is feeling queasy.*

I wonder…

CLOVE *has come close to* **ROSE** *and is sniffing her, getting closer to her belly.*

Yes.

If I didn't know better I'd say that Rose here… is carrying a child.

KING What?

CLOVE Against the law of the land.

Rose seems to be pregnant before the queen.

QUEEN *(to* **CLOVE***)* Get your hands off her.

KING Is this true Rose?

> **ROSE** *nods.*

CLOVE Your highness. You are left with no option. She must be executed.

QUEEN No.

CLOVE No one is above the law, your highness?

Not even you.

QUEEN How dare you speak to me like that.

I am your Queen.

CLOVE *(bowing deeply)* Of course.

(to **KING***)* I was merely –

QUEEN *(to* **KING***)* Well?

KING I...

I have no choice.

QUEEN You do.

The law is wrong.

The ban shall be lifted.

CLOVE Your grace –

QUEEN I said enough!

The ban will be lifted because... I am pregnant.

CLOVE Impossible!

QUEEN I beg your pardon?

CLOVE It can't be...

QUEEN What makes you so sure Clove?

> **CLOVE** *realises he's staring and looks away.*

It's funny. I feel a great curse has been lifted.

KING Is it true?

The **QUEEN** *nods, suddenly just happy.*

You're…

We're going to…

It's…

QUEEN Yes.

The **KING** *sweeps her off her feet. He runs and horses about, then remember she is pregnant and puts her down, carefully.*

It's fine.

KING I can't believe it.

We're going to have a son.

We're going to have a son.

QUEEN It might be a girl.

KING Yes. It might be a girl, but it'll be a boy. I know it.

I know it'll be a boy and we'll call him…

Pickles.

QUEEN Pickles?

Are you mad?

I'm not calling him Pickles.

KING Kingsley then.

QUEEN King Kingsley?

KING It was my favourite horse's name.

QUEEN You want to name him after a horse? Anyway, it might be a girl.

KING I don't care. I just don't care. Girl. Boy. It's wonderful.

IT'S WONDERFUL. Isn't it?

And Rose! You're pregnant too? How marvellous. How jolly… bloody marvellous!

QUEEN Language!

KING Clap!

Everyone clap.

All the advisors clap.

Look at them clapping.

All of you honk. Honk like seagulls. Like pelicans.

HONK!

They all start honking.

QUEEN Stop it.

I'm sorry your lords. His highness is overexcited.

KING I'll make them all honk. The whole world will honk for you. We're going to have a baby.

QUEEN Yes.

And now that I'm pregnant you can stop all this nonsense about a wall. We can leave the forest alone. There's no need for any of it.

The **KING** *looks like he's about to agree.*

CLOVE On the contrary your grace.

Now that the queen is pregnant. The witches will be itching to get their hands on her. They will want this baby dead.

QUEEN That's a lie! They are forbidden from killing.

CLOVE How would you know, your majesty?

KING Clove's right darling. We must be careful this time.

CLOVE She must be locked in her chambers.

QUEEN No.

KING We don't want the witches getting their hands on you.

QUEEN They're not witches.

KING It's just until the baby's born.

CLOVE And our purges of the forest must continue. Your hand must be strong and firm your highness. Until every last one of those foul women is dead.

QUEEN No. Please. You have to listen.

But the king has once more come under the influence of **CLOVE**.

CLOVE The forest ripped up.

KING The forest ripped up.

CLOVE And all the witches burned.

KING And all the witches burned.

The **QUEEN** *feels a pain in her belly. She nearly falls.*

QUEEN Oh!

CLOVE *rushes towards her.*

CLOVE Is everything okay, your majesty?

QUEEN DON'T!

Don't touch me.

CLOVE I am your physician ma'am.

QUEEN I wish to be alone.

Rose. Help me to my chambers.

CLOVE As you wish, your majesty.

The **QUEEN** *exits, beaten.* **CLOVE** *smiles.*

(trying to continue with his hypnotic voice) The wall will be finished.

KING What? Yes yes yes. But I'm going to be a father, Clove. A big, lovely, jolly Daddy. Haha!

The **KING** *chases* **CLOVE** *off in delight.*

Scene Four
The Pregnancy And Birth

FERTILITY WIFE And so the time passed, most royally.

Time expanded with the ladies.

A moon filled slowly, night by night until one morning there was an omen.

Only the queen and Rose knew what it meant.

Two pigs had given birth and died in the night. Two squealing piglets left to fend for themselves.

A sign from the fertility wife, but still the Queen did not tell the King... the promise she had made. The deal she had done. She just kept saying.

QUEEN Tomorrow. I'll definitely tell him tomorrow. I need to. I have to.

FERTILITY WIFE And so it was that little by little the promise got pushed to the back of her mind. Dwarfed by the huge expanse of her belly. The stretching and groaning. The murmurs of the king.

KING Are you okay love? Is it all okay?

FERTILITY WIFE Until finally one night the labour began and went on and on and ON until there!

A popping sound.

Just as the night was turning to day, in that in-between time, two babies were born.

Two mouths opened and sucked in the first lungful of air.

QUEEN OH

ROSE OH

KING A girl.

ROSE A girl.

QUEEN Dawn.

ROSE Eve.

QUEEN And I will love you

ROSE Forever and ever

QUEEN And nothing will take you away.

ROSE And nothing's going to come between us.

QUEEN And I will tell the king.

ROSE Everything.

QUEEN I'll tell him how I love you and how he loves you, and he won't mind the promise I made one little bit. The wall? What's the wall compared to you?

ROSE And there's something in you. I can tell that. There's something in your eyes of me. And something not.

QUEEN Something special.

ROSE Way beyond.

FERTILITY WIFE And looking in their eyes the two new mums felt a shiver run through them. And again there was an omen. A swarm of brightly coloured birds flew across the sky that no one had seen the like of before. And two of them were found in the little girls' nursery. Protecting them, who knows, but the two babies slept on.

QUEEN And still.

ROSE And still

FERTILITY WIFE And still the queen did not say.

Until it was upon them, the baby's naming day.

Scene Five
The Naming Ceremony

QUEEN Darling.

>Darling.

>There's something I need to tell you. Before the ceremony.

>Something important.

The KING *is totally engrossed by the baby, gurgling and making baby sounds.*

KING Who's a gorgeous little girlie then? Yes you are. Yes you are.

QUEEN Darling!

KING Look at her little feet.

>Aren't they gorgeous?

QUEEN I need to say about –

KING Oh! And look at her little hands. Aren't they tiny?

QUEEN I did go to the forest. Clove was right.

KING And her tiny little bellybutton.

>Yes.

>Yes it is.

QUEEN I went there and I made a promise.

KING And she's got my eyes. Definitely got my eyes.

>Wushywushywushywoo…

QUEEN I promised on our baby's life that you would leave the forest alone, you would stop building the wall. And now I'm worried it's too late. I haven't stopped a thing.

KING What's that darling?

QUEEN …

KING Oh look! She did a woopsy. Isn't that lovely?

>Daddy's going to change you.

>Yes he is. He is.

And then we're going to go and name you.

For the whole world to know.

My Princess Dawn.

My beauty.

*The **KING** goes off. The **QUEEN** slumps.*

ROSE *(to **QUEEN**)* Did you tell him, my lady?

QUEEN I couldn't, Rose. He's so happy. Look. How could I spoil that?

CLOVE Ladies and gentlemen. Welcome! Let the naming ceremony begin.

*The **KING** is beaming and clapping his hands like a kid. **DAWN**'s crib is on a podium. **EVE**'s crib is nearby or she is strapped to **ROSE**. A noise is heard, getting closer and then down from above comes an exotic bird or a balloon with a tiny basket attached. The basket is landed near **DAWN**'s cradle. **CLOVE** reads the note that accompanies each gift.*

From the outer edges of the empire. From beyond Timbuktu, a gift from the people of Poinsettia: a seed from the faraway tree. "May your daughter grow tall and strong, yet supple enough to bend in life's breezes."

KING Thank you to the kingdom of Poinsettia. We will never forget you.

A tiny whirring aeroplane now descends.

CLOVE From the watchmakers of Tick-Tock, the gift of timeliness. "May everything go like clockwork."

*A snowy white rabbit with its own aviator goggles now descends on a parachute. Round its neck is a box. **CLOVE** opens it.*

From the high mountains of the Araform comes the gift of first snow.

"May her footsteps always be soft, may she dance like the snow falling."

KING She will. I know it. Another! Another!

A kite comes in and drops another small box. **CLOVE** *opens it and the sound of a storm can be heard.*

CLOVE From the Weather Isles, a delicate breeze. "May no storm rock you. A fair wind at your back, child."

More gifts.

From the Queen of Pavlovia, a single feather from an Arctic swan. "May she be graceful and light."

We hear an elephant's call.

A trumpet from the golden elephant of the high passes. "She will have the gift of music."

KING "The gift of wit."

QUEEN *(tired)* Yes. Yes.

CLOVE From the emperor of Atatatakatatakatatakaka kakakatastan: the sands of wisdom.

KING Wealth. She will be loved by all. Won't she darling?

CLOVE May all the world know her beauty. Like the first sun's rays as she lights up the world. Princess Dawn.

KING Princess Dawn.

QUEEN *(tired)* Princess Dawn.

A squawking is heard now. Confused looks. A strange bird enters. Slightly gangly and swooping down it finally crash lands a bit and walks, not towards **DAWN**.

KING What's that?

CLOVE I don't know, your grace.

KING Where's it going?

The characters clear as the bird walks towards… **ROSE** *and kneels down.*

ROSE *looks about and undoes the message from round the bird's neck.*

ROSE *(reading)* 'There is no day without night. No Dawn without Dusk. Welcome to Eve.'

KING That's wonderful Rose. Eve got a present too. Open the box. Open it!

ROSE opens the box. The heavens crack. The **FERTILITY WIFE** *appears. The world freezes.*

FERTILITY WIFE Having a nice party?

I didn't get my invite.

Forget. Forgot. Forget me not!

Did you really think you'd get away?

The **FERTILITY WIFE** *waves her hand and the crowd part, leaving the* **QUEEN** *cowering alone.*

Well?

KING What do you want witch?

FERTILITY WIFE I came to see your girl.

KING You were not invited. You have no business here.

FERTILITY WIFE Oh, but I do.

(to the **QUEEN** *who cannot look at the* **FERTILITY WIFE***)* Will you tell him, or shall I?

It seems the queen has lost her voice.

The **FERTILITY WIFE** *goes up and squeaks in the* **QUEEN***'s face, like a scared mouse.*

KING Leave her alone.

FERTILITY WIFE I wish I had.

But it wasn't me who came a-crying when her womb was all a-barren.

Wasn't me who stalked and stumbled through the forest so forbidden.

Crying out. Help me! Help me!

Suddenly the **FERTILITY WIFE***'s voice is an exact mimic of the* **QUEEN***'s.*

"If you give me a child, I swear on its life that the king will leave you and the forest alone."

The **QUEEN** *is silent, the king is looking at her in shock.*

QUEEN *(to* **KING***)* I had to save Rose.

You would've killed her.

FERTILITY WIFE Now. I've come to collect my promise.

A baby for the forest.

KING Never.

The **FERTILITY WIFE** *approaches the* **KING***.*

FERTILITY WIFE What has happened to you?

You were once so full of hope.

You can still save her, your child.

Let life back in. Feel the sap flow.

Let the forest be. Let it flourish.

And one day you can take your daughter there. Watch her play. As you did.

KING *(the* **KING** *is moved for a second, then we see* **CLOVE***'s shadow come over him. He spits in the* **FERTILITY WIFE***'s face)*

FERTILITY WIFE Then you cannot be allowed to have this child.

It is unfair on the future.

Death must take her.

QUEEN NO!

Please! PLEASE!

I beg you.

Don't take her. Not yet.

Give us some time.

Just some time with her.

She's so beautiful.

She's all we've got.

Please.

The **FERTILITY WIFE** *pauses.*

FERTILITY WIFE Very well.

Time.

Will make it all the more painful in the end.

The **FERTILITY WIFE** *turns to the baby.*

An incantation.

"Oh little one

Oh little one

How sweet you lie beneath the sun.

15 years you'll shine for all

Don't grow too fast, don't grow too tall

Those fifteen years I give to you

Then at their end a needle true

The spindle of a spinning wheel

Will cut you down, no pain you'll feel

A little prick, that's all it takes.

For day to die and night to quake.

What is there for us to do?

When day is dead, will night be true?"

At the end of her spell **CLOVE** *breaks free. The* **FERTILITY WIFE** *sees him.*

FERTILITY WIFE You're too late. Darkness will fall.

CLOVE Fall?

After you.

CLOVE *has the ugly bird in his hands. He breaks its neck and The* **FERTILITY WIFE** *staggers back and falls into* **ROSE***'s arms.*

Your power is nothing here.

ROSE *(to* **FERTILITY WIFE***)* What about Eve?

FERTILITY WIFE What about her?

ROSE You said their fates were woven together.

FERTILITY WIFE Yes. No Day without Night. Only together will they succeed.

The **FERTILITY WIFE** *vanishes.*

The **KING***, freed, collapses.*

The **QUEEN** *goes to touch him.*

KING Get off me.

The **KING** *holds onto* **CLOVE** *instead.*

CLOVE Your majesty.

KING What've I done?

CLOVE You were not to blame sire. It was the witch.

Beat.

KING I want the forest purged, you hear me?

Every last one of them.

I want them dead.

And I want all spinning needles. No. All needles of any kind are to be banished.

CLOVE Your highness.

The **KING** *goes to exit with* **CLOVE**. **CLOVE** *stops in front of* **ROSE**.

You went with the queen to the forest, did you not?

ROSE Yes, your lordship.

CLOVE Did you have fun? Leading her majesty to the witch?

ROSE I don't understand.

CLOVE Your highness. Rose has proved herself a traitor to the king.

In league with the witches.

She must be punished.

KING Yes.

CLOVE Made an example of.

QUEEN No.

CLOVE She must be executed, your highness. Otherwise she will continue to poison the mind of the queen.

QUEEN No. You can't.

CLOVE Your lordship.

KING Do whatever you think is necessary.

CLOVE Yes, your highness. Take her away.

QUEEN It wasn't her fault. It was me.

CLOVE But your highness. You are the queen. You are above reproach.

The **QUEEN** *clings to* **ROSE** *as she is dragged off.*

QUEEN No...No! Rose!

ROSE Shhhh. You must be quiet now.

Please.

LISTEN!

You must promise to look after Eve.

The **QUEEN** *nods.*

You promise?

QUEEN Yes.

ROSE Thank you.

And please, don't tell her about any of this.

Tell her...

Tell her I was a good person.

And that I'll always love her.

Scene Six
Rose Is Executed And The Girls Grow Up

A silent dumbshow of **ROSE***'s death.*

FERTILITY WIFE A terrible day.
　A day you'll never forget.
　And yet.
　Forget it you will.
　Inevitable.
　As the sun rose and set once more.
　The two girls grew, best friends, they swore.
　'Dawn and Eve
　Day and Night'
　And the days turned to weeks turned to years turned to stone.
　While the wall got taller. The wall made strong.
　So that forest and kingdom were two not one.
　"Fifteen years you'll shine for all
　Don't grow too fast, don't grow too tall
　Those fifteen years I give to you
　Then at their end…"

Scene Seven
Preparing For The 15th Birthday Party

The castle's great hall. Everything looks gorgeous. Lights twinkling everywhere. A banner unfurls that says 'Happy 15th Birthday Princess Dawn'. Suddenly **DAWN** *runs on screaming,* **EVE** *is in hot pursuit.*

EVE Give it back.

GIVE IT BACK!

DAWN No way!

EVE Dawn!

DAWN Day!

EVE Please.

DAWN Nope. We're fifteen… nearly. It's time people saw what you actually look like instead of hiding under a hat.

EVE I like hiding under a hat.

EVE *grabs her hat back.*

DAWN Night!

It's lovely you know. Your hair.

You should show it off.

EVE Yeah right.

They see the amazing decorations all about them.

Look.

It's beautiful.

DAWN It's not bad, is it?

All for us.

EVE For you.

DAWN Hey! We're a team. Remember.

Holding out her hand.

Dawn and Eve.

Day and Night!

EVE *(give her a complicated hand shake)* "Night and Day!"

DAWN In fact…

Give me a leg-up.

EVE What?

DAWN Just give me a leg up.

EVE It's not very seemly, for a princess.

DAWN Shut up.

EVE Well, I'm just saying, now you're nearly a 'lady' you probably need to start thinking again about leg ups and stuff.

You should probably have an extendable ladder.

"Bring on the Royal Ladder".

DAWN Shhhh.

EVE "On second thoughts bring me someone I can stand on. Someone from the provinces."

DAWN Eve. I need to get this down.

EVE Why?

DAWN You'll see.

> EVE *gives* DAWN *a leg-up and the two of them manage to pull down the banner. It makes a racket and falls on* EVE *who pretends to be a zombie covered in the banner.*

(laughing) Shhhhh

Come on.

They hear the KING *off stage.*

KING *(off)* Dawn!

DAWN Dad!

Quick.

Hide it.

EVE Where?

DAWN I don't know.

EVE looks about then stuffs the banner up her jumper.

The **KING** *enters with* **CLOVE** *and a strange looking man (*PAVLOVA*) wearing a fairly strange outfit held together with pegs.*

KING Where have you been?

DAWN Just… looking.

KING I told you, you are not to be alone today.

Got it?

DAWN Sorry, Dad.

KING *(softening)* No, I'm sorry.

I know it's hard, I just…

Today is a special day.

Fifteen.

I can hardly believe it.

Look at you.

DAWN …

KING Seems like yesterday you were just my little baby. *(making baby sound)* Ooooowushywushywushywoo.

DAWN Dad.

KING And now… you're all grown up.

Hugging **DAWN** *suddenly.*

I do love you.

DAWN I know.

KING Yes…well… Dawn, this is Mr…?

PAVLOVA Pavlova.

KING Mr Pavlova.

Pavlova takes **EVE** *and looks at her.*

PAVLOVA Such beauty. Everything they say about you is true.

KING What? No. No. That's Eve.

This is my daughter.

PAVLOVA Ah yes. Beauty here too. Day and Night.

The two girls look embarassed and baffled.

Pavlova has started to examine DAWN *closely. He winks at* EVE.

Such wrists. The wrists of a swan. So fine. *(He closes his eyes and wriggles in pleasure)* Oooooooh.

DAWN What's he doing?

KING He's going to design your dress, for tonight.

DAWN What dress?

KING I know the party's not what you might've wanted. I'm sorry we can't really invite anybody, but we have to keep you safe.

DAWN It's fine, Dad.

KING But I wanted you to have a dress. And Mr Pavlova has come up with an inspirational new way of binding cloth using no needles whatsoever. Correct?

PAVLOVA No. No needles. They're so… pointy. Look! Look at me here now. Not a needle was used in the making of this gorgeous number. *(To* EVE*)* You like it?

EVE *shrugs.*

I mean look at it. Feel it feel it feel it. So smooth. So fine. You could look like this you know. It would just take a little lift here a little tuck there. *Et voila!* Mmmm. *(Pinching* EVE*'s cheek)* Gorgeous!

KING And as soon as it gets to midnight you can invite anyone you want. Have all the needles you like.

DAWN Why at midnight? Why are you so scared?

KING Oh just… superstition, darling. It's unlucky… to see a needle… before you're fifteen.

DAWN What about a dress for Eve?

EVE I'm fine.

DAWN You need something.

EVE Really Dawn. I'm fine.

KING Good. Now, off you go with Mr Pavlova.

> **DAWN** and **EVE** *make to exit.*

CLOVE Eve! The king would like you to stay a minute.

KING What? Oh... yes.

> **EVE** *stays behind. Nervous.*

Eve. You have been a true friend to my daughter.

EVE Your highness.

KING And I want to thank you for that. And I'm sure my wife would too, if she were able to. Her nerves, you know.

EVE Yes, your highness.

KING But you're both very different, Dawn has beauty, grace, wit and you... well... what I mean to say is that there comes a time when Dawn must learn to be the princess she was destined to be and you must... slip away somewhat. Oh, don't get me wrong, you will always be taken care of Eve, but where Dawn goes you will not always be able to follow.

EVE Sorry?

CLOVE After today you will no longer see Dawn.

EVE I don't understand.

CLOVE She'll be sent away to finishing school to be... finished. Free from certain..."influences"

EVE But... she's my friend.

CLOVE Yes. And your mother was a traitor.

KING You will see her again. One day. But on a different footing. Perhaps you'll get to be her maid. Now you must not tell her about our little conversation. I want you both to have a lovely time tonight, but Dawn's future is all set up. She will leave tomorrow and I don't want there to be any fuss. Do you understand?

EVE *nods her head.*

Good.

Well, enjoy and… happy birthday Eve.

The **KING** *leaves.* **CLOVE** *a moment later.*

Scene Eight
The Dress Fitting

>DAWN *is with Pavlova. She is trying on some parts of the dress.* EVE *joins them.*

DAWN What do you think?

>EVE *is not listening.*

Eve? Hello!

EVE Very nice.

DAWN What's wrong?

EVE Nothing. Just don't feel so good.

>*Beat.*

DAWN What did my dad want?

>EVE *can't look* DAWN *in the eye.*

Look! I got you this.

>DAWN *pulls out a dress.*

I thought you could wear it tonight.

EVE Me?

DAWN For when we do our dance.
You'll look great in it

EVE Maybe it's not a good idea for me to come.

DAWN What?

EVE I'll just get in the way.

DAWN Eve.
What's wrong?
You have to come.
You're the only person I'll have there.
Apart from Clove and all the staff pretending to enjoy it.

Dad's so tense he wouldn't even let me have cocktail sticks. I don't know what he thinks I'm going to do. Poke my eye out or something. It's like I'm three years old still.

Please.

We're a team. Remember! Day and Night.

Well?

EVE Night and Day.

DAWN Good.

Now try that on.

DAWN leaves. EVE, alone with Pavlova holds DAWN's dress up. She looks at herself and gives up.

PAVLOVA You are beautiful too, you know that?

EVE looks at Pavlova.

It's true.

EVE I look stupid.

PAVLOVA Only because you feel stupid. Look. It's practically seeping out of your pores. Self pity. So boring.

EVE …!

PAVLOVA Well! Don't you want to be there for your friend?

EVE nods.

So! Stop looking so flippin' miserable. Honestly, anyone would think you had little weights hanging off your mouth.

Yeees! Tiny little weights saying "I'm so sad. I'm so sad."

EVE smiles.

Look! The sun comes out. Or maybe the moon. Yes. More subtle maybe, but we all need the moon to stop us stepping in dog poo at night.

EVE laughs.

Now! Go! I will take this *(taking the dress)* and make a few alterations. Believe me. No one will recognise you.

When **EVE** *has disappeared Pavlova starts coughing. She coughs up a needle and smiles.*

Scene Nine
The 15th Birthday Party

The great hall of the castle. There is music. It's wild. A trumpet squealing. Hot jazz. The banner is back up, a bit wonky.

MASTER OF CEREMONIES *(into the microphone)* Ladies and gentlemen. The princess Dawn.

Dawn appears. She is AMAZING! Her dress is gorgeous. She starts to dance, like a kind of Charleston.

At a drumbreak in the dance **EVE** *appears. The dress* **DAWN** *gave her has been transformed into a kind of amazing suit.*

(Into mic) Ladies and gentlemen we present... Eve.

EVE *walks down the steps. She is nervous and stumbles a bit. Silence and someone laughs. Then* **DAWN** *grabs her and smiles.* **EVE** *picks herself up and looks around defiantly. The drums start again and the two do an amazing dance. It is like Fred Astaire and Ginger Rogers. HA!*

DAWN You look amazing Eve.

EVE Not so bad yourself.

CLOVE *(taps microphone, making it squeak)* Ladies and gentlemen. His royal highness.

The **KING** *takes to the microphone.*

KING Ladies and gentlemen, honoured... guest. Today is the fifteenth birthday of my beautiful daughter. And I would like to take this opportunity to give a brief overview, a sort of historical finger buffet if you will, of the kingdom that she will one day inherit. It all began with my great, great, great, great, great, great grandfather, also my second cousin twice removed, Frederick the Bloodthirsty. What an incredible man... *(the* **KING***'s speech fades to a dull monotone)*

DAWN Blah blah blah. Come on. I've set up a treat.

EVE What?

DAWN You'll see.

The two of them proceed to duck and dive around the party. They steal people's cocktails, food and generally cause mischief, then **DAWN** *gets to the corner.*

Here. Pull this.

EVE What is it?

DAWN Just do it.

EVE *pulls the lever the banner unfurls. It has been roughly altered to say 'Happy 15th Birthday Princess* **DAWN** *and* **EVE***', the bottom of it hits* **CLOVE***'s head and knocks him out. There is uproar.* **DAWN** *pulls* **EVE** *away.*

Scene Ten
A Pact To Run Away

Outside. A starlit night. **DAWN** *is a bit too hyper. She is laughing.*

EVE We shouldn't've done that.

DAWN Why not?

EVE Your dad'll kill us. You're not even supposed to be alone.

DAWN Did you see the look on old Clove's face? HA!

EVE …

DAWN What? What's wrong?

EVE Nothing.

DAWN Come on.

EVE What?

DAWN You've been acting weird all day. Ever since I left you alone with my dad. What's he said?

EVE Nothing.

DAWN Night!

EVE I can't tell you. I said I wouldn't.

DAWN Then I'll have to call on the Spanish Inquisition.

EVE You wouldn't.

> **DAWN** *grabs* **EVE** *and tickles her.*

DAWN Now tell me.

> **EVE** *is crying now.*

Eve. Hey. Hey no. I'm sorry.
What is it?

EVE It's your dad. He's sending you away.

DAWN What?

EVE He's sending you to finishing school. He said I couldn't go with you.

DAWN Over my dead body.

EVE There's nothing we can do. It's all planned out.

DAWN Is that it? Is that what you've been worried about?

EVE dries her eyes.

EVE Aren't you?

DAWN My dad's an idiot.

EVE Dawn!

DAWN It's true. I mean he's a great king and all, making the kingdom safe from witches and everything, but he's no match for me. I can twist him round my little finger. I'll just be all sad and weepy. He can't bear that.

EVE I don't think he's going to change his mind. It's Clove. I can tell it's his idea.

DAWN takes on the seriousness of the situation.

DAWN Then we'll run away.

EVE What?

DAWN We'll run away. Seriously. People do it in fairy tales all the time.

EVE Where would we go?

DAWN I don't know. The forest. Anywhere. We could live happily ever after, Eve.

DAWN gets one of the pegs off her dress and tries to cut her hand with it.

EVE What are you doing?

DAWN We have to swear a blood oath on it, but there's nothing to cut myself with.

EVE We don't need that. Just look at me.

DAWN looks at EVE. They grip hands.

I'll never leave you, Dawn.

DAWN I'll never leave you.

EVE Best friends forever?

DAWN Forever.

> *They spin around. Suddenly there is a huge sound like a thunder clap. The two are split apart. Everything turns to darkness and chaos.*

> *We see* **DAWN**. *She is in a silent space. The outside world is muffled.*

Eve! Eve!

Where are you?

What happened?

> *We hear the sound of a voice singing. It is sweet and beguiling.* **DAWN** *follows the sound.*

Scene Eleven
Eve Discovers The Curse

We are thrown into **EVE***'s world. It is chaotic. The* **KING** *runs out. The party has been destroyed.*

KING Where's Dawn?

> *Shaking* **EVE**.

> Where's Dawn?

EVE I don't know.

> She was here. Then… she was gone.

> *The* **KING** *runs off.*

KING *(shouting)* Dawn! DAWN!

> **CLOVE** *has a smile on his face.*

CLOVE Oh dear. Looks like it's happening after all.

EVE What?

CLOVE The curse.

> You see the same witch your mother was so friendly with also put a curse on little baby Dawn. To die on her fifteenth birthday.

> Oh, and listen! *(Hearing the first toll of the bell)* Only a few moments left and that curse reaches its sell-by date.

> *The strange music is in the air.* **EVE** *hears it. She runs out.*

EVE Dawn!

Scene Twelve
The Spinning Wheel

The bell continues to toll midnight. We see in slow motion **EVE** *running to find* **DAWN**. **DAWN** *is being drawn by the music until eventually a door opens in the highest turret of the castle and we see the* **FERTILITY WIFE** *spinning, making the music. The threads come from every direction so that it looks almost like a spider web or the fanned tail of some great creature. All concentrated at the point of the spinning wheel.*

The **FERTILITY WIFE** *is singing a lullaby. She sees* **DAWN** *who is entranced.*

DAWN What is it?

FERTILITY WIFE A wheel my dear.

You've never seen a spinning wheel?

Your father shouldn't have kept such things from you.

Each thread is a living thing. The wheel binds us together, sets each thread in place, until the pattern of life is made. The whole of history is in this cloth.

Every breath of every living creature.

Each leaf unfurling makes its mark.

And so we spin the future into the past.

Who knows what pattern it will make.

DAWN It's beautiful.

FERTILITY WIFE Come closer.

That's it.

Right here.

See. This is your thread. Right here.

This tiny line is you.

And it's here at this point that we are right now.

You see where the needle enters the cloth.

That's us, here now.

And now.

And now.

DAWN My thread is not very long.

FERTILITY WIFE No

> **DAWN** *is hypnotised. She comes close and reaches out.* **EVE** *runs in.*

EVE Dawn. No!

> **EVE** *causes* **DAWN** *to look up and it's then that she pricks her finger.* **DAWN***'s face registers the prick. Strange. The pain is also a pleasure. She stares at* **EVE** *and smiles. Then she collapses.*

FERTILITY WIFE "Fifteen years I gave to you

Then at their end a needle true

The spindle of a spinning wheel

Cuts you down, no pain you'll feel

A little stab, that's all it takes.

For day to die and night to quake.

What is there for us to do?

When Day is dead, will Night be true?"

EVE No.

No.

Dawn. Wake up. Wake up.

Looking at the **FERTILITY WIFE**.

What've you done?

FERTILITY WIFE Look. Her mark is in the cloth.

Her thread has ended.

Her death is woven.

EVE NO.

She will not die.

Stop it.

Stop the wheel.

FERTILITY WIFE The cloth is made. The future sewn.

It would take a great sacrifice to undo the strands, weave a different pattern.

EVE I'll do anything.

FERTILITY WIFE Really? Anything.

Just for her?

EVE *nods.*

EVE I love her.

FERTILITY WIFE To change this pattern would take a good deal of time. A thousand years.

Would you give a thousand years?

EVE Yes.

FERTILITY WIFE Are you sure? Don't underestimate how much we need our own time. You will lose everything.

EVE I'm sure.

FERTILITY WIFE Very well. The true beauty you show, to give all for another, this is the most powerful magic of all. I will remake the cloth.

An incantation.

The **FERTILITY WIFE** *takes* **EVE***'s hand and pricks it on the needle.*

The dog barks

The moon falls

A snake slips long in the grass

CLOVE *enters. He watches.*

A cat calls

But nothing to disturb

The sleep of a thousand years

A prophecy I make here.

CLOVE No.

He goes to stop her, but she flicks him away.

FERTILITY WIFE *(her voice everywhere)* HEAR ME!

> From sleep they will come from beyond the wall.
>
> Holding the key to power over all.
>
> If loved by a prince then to death one will fall.
>
> And she with true beauty will rule evermore.
>
> The forest protects these sleeping beauties.
>
> Forgotten they will be.
>
> Until from the heavens a star will come.
>
> The kiss of a prince to wake one.

> **EVE** *falls down next to* **DAWN**.

> *The* **FERTILITY WIFE** *is exhausted.* **CLOVE** *breaks free.*

> Too late.

CLOVE The king will never forgive you now. He is mine.

FERTILITY WIFE A thousand years. You have that. But the cloth has been remade. The future reset. Beauty sleeps and will come again. More powerful than us both.

CLOVE We'll see about that.

> **CLOVE** *rips out the cloth and tears it in two. The* **FERTILITY WIFE** *doubles over and disappears.*

Scene Thirteen
Time Passes And The Prince Arrives

The **KING** *enters. He picks up* **DAWN** *and moans. The bell finishes tolling midnight. Silence.*

FERTILITY WIFE And so it begins. The silence that will last a thousand years.

Sleep you

Sleep you

We protect you

Stars fall

Day dawns

Still you sleep you

Turning

Spinning

Forest forming.

Growing over

Things forgotten

Sleep you

Sleep you

We protect you

Till the time that is a coming

One day

One day

Hear it coming…

Hope lies waiting

Beauty sleeping

Till the day that is a-coming…

During the lullaby we see time begin to pass in a dumbshow.

The **KING** *puts on a hat of shame. It is shaped like a huge tall dunce's cap and on each hand is also a conical cap. He wanders around the castle, an old man now, shuffling in the shadows of his once-great kingdom. Slowly the dust sheets are put on everything and slowly, slowly it all settles. The* **KING** *sits on his throne, still at last. His crown falls and rolls. We see* **CLOVE** *pick it up, place it on his own head and walk out through the audience. And over everything a fine dust settles. The castle is abandoned and a great forest of thorns grows up around it. We see that elsewhere, far away, spring up houses and a railway; the beginnings of a city.. Time passes. As the future progresses the tower that the two girls lie in becomes a bower, rocked gently by the breeze in the branches.*

Crowds come and go in the now growing city. And over it all we hear the speeches of **CLOVE**. *Great speeches that proclaim the future. How everyone will be bright and beautiful and can live perfect lives in the city. How everyone needs to bow down to the great leader. And in the sky the stars burn down bright. Unchanging. Until a great meteor sparks into life and travels across the sky. No one knows what it means, but it is seen as a great omen. And as the meteor passes overhead we are drawn into the bower of the sleeping beauties and a spark can be seen there. A crackle of life.*

We hear the incantation of the **FERTILITY WIFE** *and suddenly a small chink of light appears in the wall behind them. A light shines through. The hole is suddenly bigger as the back layer of undergrowth is torn away and a man is revealed. He looks like a spaceman, so far from the future is he. But a strange spacemen with elements of the knight in shining armour about him. And possibly roller skates. He rips down the rest of the wall and comes into the room, a silhouette against the bright light surrounding him.*

He takes off his helmet. He is GORGEOUS!

He stares into the room and then sees **DAWN**, *lying there. His breath is taken away.*

He sees her and cannot help it. He is drawn to her. We hear the prophesy whispered "The kiss. The kiss. The kiss to wake one" He puts his hand out to touch her then leans down and kisses her.

A moment and **DAWN** *awakes. They stare at one another. Lovestruck.*

DAWN You.

PRINCE Yes.

There is a movement behind the prince and **EVE** *sits up.*

EVE Oi! What do you think you're doing?

EVE *bashes the* **PRINCE** *on the head with a stick and he falls down.*

DAWN Eve!

EVE What happened?

I had the strangest dream.

***

Interval

ACT II

SCENE ONE
Time Has Passed

The Bower. **EVE** *and* **DAWN** *are standing over the prince.*

EVE Who is he?

ABC What was he doing to you?

DAWN Nothing.

EVE He was attacking you.

DAWN …

EVE You can't trust strange men.

Abc Especially not ones with blonde hair.

This can be altered to suit the actor's hair.

DAWN Shhh. He's coming round.

The prince wakes up.

Again he stares straight at **DAWN**.

He smiles.

She smiles.

EVE *watches.*

EVE What do you want?

PRINCE Sorry?

EVE Who are you?

DAWN Eve!

EVE What?

Look at him. He's obviously not right.

The **PRINCE** *lets out a laugh.*

What?

What's so funny?

PRINCE Nothing.

It's just, your clothes.

DAWN What?

PRINCE I've just never seen clothes like that before.

EVE You can talk. Look at you. What are you meant to be? The Pied Piper?

DAWN Eve!

(To **PRINCE***)* Sorry.

My name's Dawn.

This is –

PRINCE Eve.

DAWN Yeah

EVE Don't tell him our names.

He might…

DAWN What?

EVE He might be playing mind games. Look! He's trying to hypnotise you. Don't look in his eyes.

DAWN I'm afraid my friend hit you on the head.

PRINCE I know. Good reflexes.

EVE Thank you. I do have good reflexes, and don't you forget it. I could kill you at a thousand paces.

PRINCE How?

EVE What?

PRINCE How? At a thousand paces. That's quite far.

EVE Yes. But some of us have it and some of us don't. Just remember that.

PRINCE I will.

DAWN So…

What's your name?

PRINCE Oh, sorry.

I'm Prince.

EVE Prince?

PRINCE Yes.

EVE What kind of a name is that?

PRINCE My name.

EVE Prince? Sounds like a dog's name.

DAWN It's a good name.

PRINCE Thank you.

EVE What have you done with us?

PRINCE I'm sorry?

EVE Where are we?

PRINCE I don't know.

EVE What?

What kind of a person are you?

You don't know where you are?

PRINCE No.

I mean I do, but this isn't supposed to be here.

EVE What are you talking about?

PRINCE I was following the star.

EVE He's off his trolley. I think we should ignore him.

DAWN What star?

PRINCE A star appeared in the heavens one month ago.

No one knew what it was.

It's not on any astronomical maps. I checked. All of them.

People said it was an omen.

So I followed it.

Strange. I wouldn't normally do that. I wouldn't normally trust in things like that. But, I don't know, I just felt this pull. Like my own self was off balance. Do you know what I mean?

DAWN ...yes.

PRINCE Two days ago I passed beyond the outer limits. And then... I must've fallen asleep or something and when I woke up there was this forest, then here *(looking in* **DAWN***'s eyes)* then you.

EVE What's he talking about?

DAWN What are the outer limits?

PRINCE Beyond the wall, that separates our world from the old places.

DAWN And we are beyond that wall?

PRINCE Yes.

Which is strange.

No one is supposed to be out here.

The forest, the tower surrounded by thorns.

I had to hack my way in.

Whose tower is it?

DAWN I don't know.

DAWN *looks around.*

But I recognise it.

Don't you Eve?

EVE It's creepy.

I've read about this sort of thing.

He's kidnapped us and brought us here to... who knows what. He's probably got an enchanted...flute or something.

He'll try and charm us with some dwarves in a minute.

DAWN Look.

> DAWN *parts some of the undergrowth that has grown over everything. She finds some material with a symbol woven into it.*

It's our crest.

My family crest.

Look.

EVE Dawn.

I'm not sure…

I think we should leave this place.

It's not right.

DAWN Wait.

> DAWN *uncovers the cloth. It leads to the feet of a skeleton. Two skeletons are revealed wearing robes made of the cloth.*

> DAWN *approaches, she touches a skeleton and it collapses a bit. They all jump.*

Father.

Mother.

The skeletons crumble to dust.

> EVE *goes to comfort* DAWN. DAWN *pulls away and starts pulling down some more of the undergrowth.*

EVE Dawn.

DAWN What's going on?

I said WHAT'S GOING ON?!

> DAWN *has revealed the crumbling walls of their tower room. The ceiling has gone and the stars are revealed. A full moon.*

We're in the tower, Eve.

What's happened?

Where's the rest of the castle?

EVE I don't know.

DAWN Look. It's dark.

EVE What?

DAWN There should be houses there.

> The village.
>
> It's all gone.
>
> …
>
> What's happened to us?

EVE … a thousand years.

DAWN What?

EVE That's what she said.

DAWN Who?

EVE That's impossible.

DAWN What? Eve!

EVE It was your birthday, remember?

DAWN *(remembering)* … yeah.

EVE I found you. There was a woman. She was spinning a huge cloth and she said you were going to die.

> She said the only way to save you was if a thousand years passed.

DAWN That's impossible.

EVE I know.

> But look.
>
> The castle's crumbled.

DAWN *(to* **EVE***)* What are we going to do?

EVE I don't know.

> **EVE** *sees* **DAWN** *'s distress.*
>
> We'll be okay.
>
> We'll live here.
>
> Night and Day.
>
> **DAWN** *is silent.*

What?

DAWN There's nothing left.

EVE We can hunt for food.
Live in the forest.

DAWN I don't know.

PRINCE I think it's quite hard. Hunting. You have to know how to set snares and things.

DAWN Do you?

PRINCE Yeah. And how to do tiny knots.

EVE I can do tiny knots.

PRINCE And how to make a bivouac.

DAWN A what?

PRINCE It's like a shelter made of leaves. I read about it.

DAWN Oh.

EVE That's fine too. I know all about that stuff. We'll be fine.

PRINCE Right.

EVE In fact, if there's nothing else…

PRINCE Right. Yes.
I suppose I should go then.

DAWN Oh.

EVE Yes. That would be a good idea.

PRINCE Right.
I'll go back through the deep dark forest.
Alone.

EVE Yes.

PRINCE Right.

EVE Good.

PRINCE Yes.

EVE *(indicating the door)* I think it's…

PRINCE Yes.

*The **PRINCE** is slowly making to go. **DAWN** is looking at him.*

Unless…

DAWN What?

PRINCE Well, if you've got nowhere else then you could come back with me.

To the city.

I'm sure she wouldn't mind.

EVE Who?

PRINCE My mother.

The Queen of Everything.

She's not my real mother, she adopted me when I was little. But she'd love you. I know she would.

And I could show you the city and the palace and *(indicating his roller-skates)* how to use wheels.

EVE *is about to laugh with* **DAWN**, *then she sees* **DAWN**'s *face.*

EVE You're not serious.

DAWN Why not?

EVE Because… Because he's a lunatic.

(to **PRINCE***)* You followed a star, right?

PRINCE *nods.*

See!

He's completely mad.

He'll make us follow a squirrel next, or some fog.

Is that what you want?

To follow some fog until we're all…

(Seeing **DAWN** *staring at the* **PRINCE** *she lets out a puff of frustration)*
Umph!

DAWN Please Eve.

I can't go without you.

Pause.

EVE FINE!

Fine. We'll go with him.

(To **PRINCE***)* But I'm warning you. Any funny business. If you even *look* like you're going to do something funny, I'll kill you.

PRINCE From a thousand paces?

EVE Exactly!

Scene Two
The Glowworms

Night time. The forest. **EVE**, **DAWN** *and the* **PRINCE** *are settling down for the night. Creepy forest sounds all around. An owl.*

PRINCE What was that?

EVE Just an owl.

Another noise.

PRINCE And that?

EVE Just a bat.

Another noise.

PRINCE And that?

EVE That was my patience snapping.

   Why are you so jumpy?

PRINCE I've never seen so many trees before.

EVE Really?

PRINCE The forests were all cut down eons ago. This must be the last one left. I never thought I'd get to see it. Listen. It's like the trees are speaking.

EVE They are. If you listen carefully. They hold every secret ever told.

DAWN Who told you that?

EVE Just... it's what they used to say in the kitchens.

DAWN Why don't you tell us a story, Prince? From where you come from. Something to help us sleep.

PRINCE What?

DAWN A story.

EVE You don't know what a story is?

DAWN You know, like Little Red Riding Hood. Or The Three Musketeers.

EVE Or Big Sausage, Little Sausage.

PRINCE I don't know what you mean.

DAWN You must have stories.

PRINCE You mean about how the queen is everything. How there is nothing beyond the wall.

DAWN I don't think so.

PRINCE You tell me one. A "story".

DAWN What about Beauty and the Beast?

EVE Yes!

DAWN Once Upon a Time.

PRINCE *(enchanted already)* "Once Upon a Time".

DAWN Yeah.

EVE It means a long time ago, you idiot.

DAWN Once upon a time…

> *Suddenly the* **FERTILITY WIFE** *appears.* **EVE** *jumps up. The other two are oblivious to her.*

EVE Who's there?

FERTILITY WIFE Don't you recognise me?

I came to see how you are after your little nap.

EVE *(indicating* **PRINCE** *and* **DAWN***)* What have you done to them?

FERTILITY WIFE They simply can't see the things you can.

You're very perceptive, Eve. Amazingly so.

EVE What do you want, witch?

FERTILITY WIFE I came to say that I'm sorry for what happened to you.

EVE It was *your* fault.

FERTILITY WIFE It must seem that way to you, but you know a bigger pattern can't always be seen close up.

EVE I don't want a bigger pattern.

I want to go back.

FERTILITY WIFE Can't.

You gave all that up for Dawn. You don't regret that do you? Saving her?

EVE ... No.

FERTILITY WIFE Remember that. No matter what happens. On your friendship the future rests.

The **FERTILITY WIFE** *holds out a pendant.*

Take this.

EVE What is it?

FERTILITY WIFE We are in the last remaining bit of forest. I have used all my powers to keep it hidden from the queen. When you need me most this will show you the way back.

EVE You! I'll never need you.

FERTILITY WIFE Believe me. One day you will need a friend and when that day comes we will be here for you.

EVE *considers the pendant, then takes it. The* **FERTILITY WIFE** *disappears.* **EVE** *is left confused.* **DAWN** *has reached the end of her story.*

DAWN ... and so he was transformed into a handsome prince and the two of them were married and lived truly happy forever after. The end.

PRINCE *(overcome)* Amazing. You're amazing, Dawn.

DAWN *(noticing* **EVE** *standing)* Eve. Are you okay?

EVE Yeah. Did you...?

DAWN Oh look. Glow-worms.

PRINCE *(suddenly noticing the lights all around them. Scrambling up, scared)* What are they?

DAWN It's fine. They must have come out to hear the story.

They watch as the glow-worms start to make a sound.

PRINCE What are they doing?

DAWN Singing. They sing to say thank you.

(she sings) "You're welcome".

PRINCE The forest. It's beautiful. I never knew.

EVE It is.

They watch as the whole forest lights up and sings.

FERTILITY WIFE Now sleep.

All of you.

You have a long journey ahead.

The three of them fall asleep and the stage is transformed into the city.

Now two girls so young

Kept you safe for so long

How can we see you go?

All of our hope lies with you

Lies with not one but two

With the love that you show.

Confusion and doubt

Will find you out.

Nothing can be as it was

For as the world turns

So do we learn

That we don't always get what we want.

Remember love

Remember the woods

For the big bad world

Won't always be good

So remember the trees

Wherever you go
Our hope lies with you
And the love you show.

Scene Three
Queenie Meets Dawn And Eve

The **QUEEN** *storms on with her henchmen,* **POKE** *and* **BONE**. *She is furious. Around her are whispers of the prophecy. They are like flies to her. Irritants.*

QUEENIE I want him FOUND!

POKE Yes, your highness.

BONE We've tried, your highness.

QUEENIE Well, you obviously haven't tried hard ENOUGH. HAVE YOU!?

BONE No, your worshipfullness.

QUEENIE How did you let him get away?

POKE It was at the wall, your highness. He went over it.

QUEENIE What?

BONE Just climbed it. In those wheels of his. We didn't know what to do.

QUEENIE You should've stopped him.

BONE We were going to but… we got distracted. By the star. Couldn't stop staring at it.

QUEENIE Enough of this star. I want no more talk of it. Any conversation about the star will be punishable by death. Understood?

POKE Yes, your highness.

BONE What about the birds?

QUEENIE What?

BONE People have been seeing birds, your grace. Brightly coloured ones.

QUEENIE …

BONE And someone said they saw a flower today. Growing wild in the fountains. They said it was beautiful.

QUEENIE Who said that?

BONE A child.

QUEENIE I want that child found. It must not be allowed to spread. This insurrection. The flower will be pulled out and made an example of. All birds will be shot on sight. In fact shoot anything that moves. Flowers, rabbits, children. They do not exist. Understood?

BONE AND POKE Yes your grace.

QUEENIE There is no beauty, but me. There is nothing beyond the wall. I am the Queen of Everything.

> **PRINCE** *enters with* **DAWN** *and* **EVE**. **QUEENIE** *immediately grabs* **PRINCE**.

DARLING!

Oh baby baby baby. My baby.

PRINCE Mother.

QUEENIE What's happened to you? Where have you been?

PRINCE I went to follow the star.

QUEENIE I was worried sick. My baby.

> *She sees his clothes and is horrified.*

What's this? Your clothes. They're covered.

PRINCE It's mud. Isn't it amazing?

QUEENIE Mud. Get them off. Get them off! I want them burned. Hear me? All of them!

PRINCE Mother.

I want you to meet my friends.

This is Dawn and Eve.

> *To* **DAWN** *and* **EVE**.

This is her highness. The Queen of Everything.

> **QUEENIE** *looks at them. She is astonished. She feels sick, but tries to hide it.* **DAWN** *hesitates, then curtsies.*

DAWN Pleased to meet you, your highness.

> EVE *is staring at* QUEENIE. *Then she looks down and curtsies too.*

QUEENIE How…
You.

PRINCE I found them, mother.
Beyond the wall.
They were in an old castle surrounded by forest.

> BONE *gasps.*

QUEENIE There is no more forest. I've killed it.

PRINCE I found one last bit.
It was amazing. All the things inside, the animals, the trees.
And then I found Dawn and Eve. Asleep.

> *Another gasp.*

QUEENIE Enough! I mean… I feel… *(She goes to faint.* POKE *goes to catch her, but she bats him off. Staring at* DAWN*)* This can't be. You were…
What do you want here?

DAWN Your highness. We had nowhere to go and Prince kindly said we could come back with him. If it's a problem then we'll leave as soon as possible.

EVE Good.

PRINCE You can't leave.
Mother, please, I said they could stay.
Dawn is a princess.

DAWN Was.

EVE Is.

QUEENIE Really? A princess?
It's funny. There was an old folk tale about a princess. Sleeping beyond the wall.

BONE The prophecy.

> **POKE** *kicks* **BONE** *to shut him up.*

QUEENIE But no one could ever find her.
No matter how hard they tried.
And believe me, they tried.
Until it seemed she must be dead.

EVE Well now we're back.

QUEENIE Yes.

> …

And here you must stay. In fact we wouldn't dream of letting you out of our sight.
My sleeping beauty.
A forest, you say?
I don't suppose you met anyone else while you were there?

PRINCE Only some glow-worms.

QUEENIE They say witches lived there once.

> *The* **QUEEN** *is staring at* **EVE**. **EVE** *drops her eyes.*

Yes. You must stay and tell me all about it.
I insist.

> *Suddenly there is a noise from above. A honking.*

PRINCE What's that?

> *Everyone looks up and gasps.*

BONE *(terrified)* Geese! Geese!
Get down.
Protect the queen.

> *He goes to jump on the* **QUEEN**. *She pushes him off.*

PRINCE It's fine. They're flying away.

> **PRINCE** *stares at them, a smile of amazement on his face.*

EVE What's the problem? They're just geese.

PRINCE There haven't been birds here for a very long time.

They're beautiful.

QUEENIE Enough!

You must show the girls to the guest rooms.

They must be tired. And you'll want to get out of those old rags.

The Pig Ball is in a few days and it would be wonderful if you could both be there.

DAWN, EVE and PRINCE exit. The QUEEN turns to POKE.

I want those birds dead and stuffed.

POKE Yes, your highness.

QUEENIE Pretty pretty girl isn't she?

BONE Beautiful!

POKE Nothing compared to you, your highness.

The QUEEN strokes POKE's face.

QUEENIE Really?

You'll keep an eye on them, won't you? I wouldn't want them to leave the city. *(Her stroke turns to a strangle)* Or it'll be you I have stuffed.

The QUEEN exits.

POKE notices BONE cowering on the floor.

He pulls him upright.

POKE What are you doing?

BONE You heard it. "From sleep they will come from beyond the wall." It's them. We're doomed.

POKE Enough.

BONE And the geese and the flower in the fountain. It's a sign. The prophecy. It's true!

POKE *(squeezing* **BONE***'s nose)* I said shut up you idiot. If the Queen hears you she'll have both our insides strung out for the crows.

BONE There aren't any crows.

POKE No. And we're here to keep it that way. Got it. Starting with those geese. Now, come on!

They exit.

Scene Four
The Palace And The Facemakers

EVE, DAWN *and* PRINCE *enter.*

PRINCE So that's pretty much the east wing of the palace.

DAWN Really? How many wings are there?

PRINCE I don't know. It's always being extended. Over five hundred.

EVE *groans loudly.*

Maybe that's enough sightseeing for today though. Unless... I could show you the fountains later, if you want.

DAWN *is about to agree.*

EVE No thanks! I think we've had enough to last us for about... forever.

I mean it's all so... weird.

PRINCE Really?

DAWN I didn't think so.

EVE Why were all those people on stilts?

PRINCE They're not stilts, they're shoes. They're actually lower this year. Last year someone fell off theirs and died, so out of respect the fashion houses have brought them down a bit, for now.

EVE And the trees. They're all so tiny?

PRINCE So they can be shaped. To look like the queen.

EVE *(realising)* Ahhh. I thought they were just lumpy.

DAWN I think it's amazing. Everything's so bright.

EVE Really?

DAWN Everything's so dark where we're... where we were from. All candle-lit.

EVE You like candles.

DAWN They're a bit gloomy.

EVE Really?

Suddenly two people rush on. They are the facemakers. Highly fashionable. Like gorgeous, pure breed hens.

SANDÉ There you are. There you are.

JOILÉ My GOD! We've been looking everywhere for you.

SANDÉ Oh my goodness. It's too much.

It's too much.

Isn't it too much?

JOILÉ It is too much.

It's a lot.

I'll grant you that. A lot it is, but then…

TOGETHER That's what we were born for.

JOILÉ A challenge.

SANDÉ *(appraising* **DAWN***)* Oooh, I like your eye. You have a really good left eye. That could definitely work to your advantage.

JOILÉ *(appraising* **EVE***)* Shame. Still. We'll do our best.

SANDÉ We can erase the rest, but that eye… I think…yes… I love it.

The two facemakers start to pinch and prod the girls.

EVE What are you doing? Get off. GET OFF ME!

JOILÉ Oooooooooh

PRINCE It's okay. Eve, Dawn, these are the facemakers. They're here to help.

BOTH We make you shine

We make you glow

So

Why waste beauty on the inside?

JOILÉ Right. I think we need to start with a serious braiding session.

We can braid all your hair. Your eyebrows, your teeth. A tuck there, a little nip there. *Et voila!*

EVE I said get OFF!

JOILÉ *falls to the ground.*

JOILÉ AAAhhhhh. She hurt me.

She hurt me!

EVE I didn't touch him.

JOILÉ Look at her. Naughty girl. Naughty NAUGHTY GIRL. Stuff her mouth. Stuff it up with soil!

SANDÉ Joilé! Control yourself.

Now. *(To* **DAWN***)* What about you? What kind of skin would you like?

DAWN I'm sorry?

SANDÉ A skin. A skin. "Love the skin you're in."

PRINCE They're not from round here.

SANDÉ I can see that.

PRINCE People here have what they call skins. They're really thin and you put them over your face.

EVE What for?

SANDÉ Because they're pretty.

JOILÉ And they stop you looking old. You'd never guess she was a hundred and five.

SANDÉ *(Giving* **JOILÉ** *daggers, then back to* **DAWN***)* Look. Do you like mine?

DAWN Yeah.

EVE Seriously?

DAWN Look Eve. *(Looking at* **SANDÉ***'s face)* Your skin shines.

SANDÉ I know. It's extremely expensive. It's called Glamourpuss.

Oh we are going to have so much fun getting you ready.

EVE What for?

SANDÉ For the Pig Ball.

It's so much fun.

AHHHHH!

I can't wait.

Can you wait?

I can't wait.

JOILÉ And what am I meant to do with this one?

I suppose we could do something with your hair. Maybe use it to cover your face.

EVE I'm fine thanks.

I don't want anything.

JOILÉ Fine.

I know when I'm not wanted.

…

So, you definitely don't want me?

EVE No.

JOILÉ Good. That's what I thought.

SANDÉ starts to make over **DAWN** *and* **JOILÉ** *tries to do* **EVE** *who is having none of it. The lights fade over the following speech.*

SANDÉ *(trailing off)* Now just remember the rules. They're strictly enforced.

No running about, it ruins your complexion.

No smiling. Wrinkles.

If you have to eat then put the food far away from you. That way you burn off more calories than you take in. Celery is good.

Don't eat cakes.

Make sure to look bored most of the time. That's great for keeping your face young.

Look! There! That's my normal look now. I was a terrible child, always smiling. They teach you not to. I was always forgetting though, so they stuck me in a room once, pinned open my eyes and played horror flicks until I could never smile again.

It's brilliant.

I won't tell you my age, but let's just say I remember when there were still seasons. Before they blocked them out. They're terrible for your complexion. Did you know that? All that change in pressure and humidity. It was better once they'd built the giant dome over everything. I never go out now.

Apparently the sun still shines, but not many people look at it now.

It's more just for photographs and stuff. They superimpose the sun.

Nice.

You're going to love it here.

Scene Five
Echo

The **QUEEN***'s nest, somewhere deep in the castle. In the air are whispers of the prophecy.*

WHISPERS From sleep they will come.

From sleep they will come.

Wiser than their...

Older than their...

She who has beauty...

Rule evermore.

They press in on the **QUEEN** *until she can't take it any more.*

QUEENIE *Enough!*

She draws back a curtain. Behind is a looking glass.

Mirror mirror on the wall. Who's the fairest of them all?

*In the mirror an old man (***ECHO***) appears. He is broken and ruined. He has been trapped here a long time. Where his eyes should be are only holes.*

Tell me.

ECHO Not you.

A greater beauty now rests within the palace walls.

QUEENIE Yes.

ECHO "From sleep they will come from beyond the wall.

Holding the key to power over all."

QUEENIE Enough.

ECHO "If loved by a prince then to death one will fall.

And –"

QUEENIE I said ENOUGH!

The **QUEEN** *electrocutes* **ECHO** *and he falls in pain.*

You keep giving me pain.

ECHO I am simply your Echo. I am a part of you.

QUEENIE You are a blind old man.

ECHO The last bit of truth you have left.

The prophecy has arrived.

Your reign is at an end.

QUEENIE Never.

Did you think I would not have prepared for this?

A thousand years I've waited.

Bringing up that disgusting Prince. "Mother! Oh mummy! Eugh."

You think I would be beaten by a girl?

I don't think so.

"If married to a prince then to death one will fall.

And she with true beauty will rule evermore."

Very well.

Let the prophecy come.

I am ready for it.

Scene Six
Getting Ready For The Pig Ball

The night of the Pig Ball. We can hear muffled music coming from somewhere in the palace. **EVE** *is sitting alone in* **DAWN**'s *dark room. She has* **DAWN**'s *old dress in her hand. Looking at it.*

DAWN *enters.*

DAWN Oh, Eve! You gave me a fright.

What are you doing sitting in the dark?

EVE I was waiting for you.

We said we'd meet. Remember? Get ready for the ball.

Beat.

DAWN I forgot.

I'm sorry.

EVE It's fine.

I was just worried about you, that's all. I haven't seen you for days.

DAWN I know.

I've been hanging out with Prince.

He's shown me the whole place. Even the map room. It's off limits, but he knows a way in. There are maps and books everywhere.

And look!

Pointing at some roller-skates she is wearing.

He's been giving me lessons.

Yesterday I fell right into him. I felt such an idiot, but he just smiled, you know that way. And he held me…there… for ages.

He's so great Eve.

Don't you think he's great?

Seeing **EVE**'s *reaction.*

What?

EVE Well, don't you think he's a bit…

Don't you think you should cool it a bit.

I mean guys like you to play hard to get, right?

DAWN Do they?

EVE Yeah.

Really hard. You should probably ignore him. Maybe even hit him… hard… on the face.

I reckon he'd fall for that.

…

Have you kissed him yet?

DAWN No.

EVE Right.

DAWN Do you think I should?

EVE No!

I mean… I don't know.

DAWN What's wrong?

EVE Nothing.

It's just…

Don't you miss home?

DAWN *looks away.*

EVE I keep hearing things. At night. Like someone crying in the walls. Do you hear that?

DAWN You've just got to try and not think about it. Home, I mean. That's what I do. Like they say "No one likes a sad person."

EVE Who says?

DAWN And besides, there is nowhere else, Eve. This is it. The future.

EVE We could escape. Live like outlaws.

Putting her hand out.

Night and Day!

DAWN *(not responding to the handshake)* We can't really though, can we?

I mean that was just kids' stuff.

Seeing **EVE** *is hurt.*

You just need to have a good night.

Look! I got these *(pulling out some piggy ears and two pig noses)* For the ball tonight.

EVE I'm not wearing that.

DAWN You have to.

All the girls dress as little piggies and the guys dress as wolves.

Then at midnight they turn the lights out and we all get ravaged.

EVE That's ridiculous.

I'll ravage them if they even try and touch me.

DAWN Come on!

It'll be fun.

Look. We just need to sort your hair out.

Adjusting **EVE**, *pulling her hair up etc.*

There.

And this *(she takes* **EVE**'s *top off one shoulder)*

And smile.

EVE *can't help herself from smiling, embarrassed at* **DAWN**'s *attention.*

There.

Beautiful.

EVE Really?

EVE *stares at* DAWN. *It is a bit too intense.* DAWN *looks away.*

What time shall we go?

DAWN Oh… I said I'd meet Prince.

He's going to walk me in.

EVE Right.

DAWN You could come too.

EVE No.

DAWN You *could*.

EVE No.

I'll be fine.

Scene Seven
The Pig Ball

The music kicks in. It is similar to the music from the 15th birthday party, but a thousand years on. Wild! Half the cast are piggies and half are wolves. They do the Piggie Wolf dance. At a drum break **DAWN** *dances a solo just like the first half,* **EVE** *is about to join her, but gets spun off so that* **PRINCE** *can partner* **DAWN**. *Alone* **EVE** *watches, then leaves the party.*

Scene Eight
Eve Finds Echo And A Spell Is Cast

EVE *sits alone.*

She hears something in the walls.

Someone crying.

She listens.

EVE Hello?

ECHO Hello.

EVE Is someone there?

ECHO Is someone there?

Echo.

Help us.

Please.

Help.

EVE *gets lower and lower in the castle.*

Darker and darker until she finds the **QUEEN***'s nest. She pulls back the curtain and there is* **ECHO***.*

Beauty.

EVE I'm Eve.

ECHO I hear beauty in your voice.

EVE Who are you?

ECHO Echo.

EVE Why are you locked up?

ECHO Been here a long long time.

Locked up. Chained up. Since ever I was made.

EVE Why?

ECHO Because I see too much.

To do great evil you must get rid of a part of yourself. The part that sees. Lock it up. Chain it away.

That is me.

Echo.

But I still see. In my own small way.

You shine Eve. Your love for Dawn is strong. You must not lose that.

EVE She's changed.

ECHO Trust her. You are still Night and Day.

EVE What happened to your eyes?

ECHO He took them.

EVE Who?

There is a noise. The **QUEEN** *approaching.*

ECHO Hide.

She must not find you.

HIDE!

EVE *goes to run, but the* **QUEEN** *is nearly upon them.* **EVE** *hides.*

The **QUEEN** *enters.*

QUEENIE So…

Still whittering to yourself old man.

I thought you'd like to see this.

The **QUEEN** *has a box.*

She opens it and inside is an apple.

She stares at it.

Fruit from the first tree.

Yes.

Beautiful, isn't it.

And yet. It will be deadly.

ECHO What've you done?

QUEENIE Nothing yet.

It's what *you're* about to do that matters.

I need your magic.

ECHO Don't do this.

QUEENIE What?

ECHO The more you use me the weaker I become.

QUEENIE Yes.

ECHO I am still a part of you.

QUEENIE But you're an old and ugly man.

How can you be part of me?

And yet, it seems you are.

…

My soul.

The **QUEEN** *has taken off her wig. She has changed so we can see she is* **CLOVE**.

EVE *gasps.*

The **QUEEN** *stops still, listening.*

She swivels her head about.

She starts to move towards where **EVE** *is hiding.*

ECHO What is the spell you require?

QUEENIE The Spell of The End.

ECHO It's too great.

I won't survive.

QUEENIE No.

But then, I won't be needing you again.

ECHO It's not too late.

QUEENIE For what?

ECHO For you. You were once a good man. A great wizard. The forest would take you back, you know. Even now.

QUEENIE Is that what you think I want?

To dance amongst the trees again?

…

My sweet Echo.

All these years I've kept you.

The last link to what I once was. The pathetic magic of the forest.

But to fulfill the prophecy I must give all.

Even you.

There must be nothing left of me.

Then I can truly become beauty.

The QUEEN *begins chanting a spell.*

The apple glows.

ECHO *(to* EVE*)* Go.

GO!

As the QUEEN *gets lost in her spell.* EVE *runs away unseen.*

QUEENIE I call on all that is dark.

Hear me.

I give you the final part of me.

And invoke the spell of the end.

We see ECHO *glowing as the last of his power is used up for the spell.*

Whoever bites the apple shall die.

And with it shall I

Inherit their soul.

All their beauty will be mine and no more Queen will I be.

But ruler of all eternally.

The **QUEEN** *casts the spell.*

ECHO *dies.*

The apple turns red.

It is evil.

The mirror cracks.

Behind the glass lies **ECHO**, *dead.*

The **QUEEN** *turns him over with her foot.*

Looks at him a second.

Then she walks out.

Scene Nine
A Near Kiss And A Fight

PRINCE and DAWN are alone.

PRINCE takes off DAWN's pig mask.

She takes off his wolf mask.

DAWN That was fun.

PRINCE Yeah. I've never been to the Pig Ball before.

I always thought it sounded dumb, but… dancing with you well… it was great.

DAWN Me too.

I mean, dancing with you.

They are close.

PRINCE Dawn, I…

DAWN *(simultaneously)* Do you think…

PRINCE Sorry, after you.

DAWN I was just going to say, do you think this could last forever?

PRINCE Me too… I mean, yeah.

DAWN Prince.

PRINCE Yes.

DAWN I…

They are about to kiss when EVE barges between them.

EVE Quick.

Quick.

We have to go.

DAWN Eve!

EVE Seriously.

There is some weird stuff going down in this palace and we do *not* want to be part of it.

DAWN I was talking to Prince.

EVE So?

DAWN *(exasperated)* So…

EVE Dawn. I was just down below, in the dungeons somewhere. There's someone called Echo. Being kept prisoner in a mirror and then the Queen came in and I finally realised where I recognised her from. It's Clove. The Queen is Clove. She took her wig off and –

DAWN Eve. This really isn't a good time.

EVE What?

Can't you hear me?

DAWN Yes. And I'm sorry, but I'm not up for playing games right now.

EVE I'm not.

DAWN Going on about Clove.

He's gone. A long time ago.

EVE I know, he should be, but… I think he's a witch.

DAWN Look. We can talk about it later.

EVE We have to go now.

DAWN No.

I'm not going.

I'm dancing with Prince.

I'm sorry if…

EVE What?

DAWN I'm sorry if it makes you jealous.

EVE Jealous? Of you?

DAWN Yes.

EVE You must be joking.

I just feel sorry for you.

Going with that total idiot. "Oooh, Princey this and Princey that. I wonder what Princey will think". Can't you see how stupid you look?

There are things going on in this palace. Terrible things and here you all are dancing like a bunch of idiots with your piggie face and your stupid grin. You look like a clown.

DAWN Eve.

EVE You do. All of you. You all look stupid.

DAWN Where are you going?

EVE Why do you care? You're not my friend. Night and Day? It's kids' stuff.

EVE *exits.*

DAWN *is about to run after her when the* QUEEN *catches her and stops her.*

QUEENIE Ladies and gentlemen.

So good to see so many of you here at the Pig Ball.

Ladies?

The girls all oink.

Gents?

The men all growl.

And now. A very special announcement.

Dawn. It seems you have stolen my little Princey's heart. Right from under my very nose.

And so I've given in to love and would like to announce to the whole kingdom the upcoming marriage of Prince and Dawn.

The daughter I always longed for.

What do you say?

DAWN *looks lost for words.*

PRINCE Marriage?

QUEENIE Of course, my darling. Dawn must be married to a prince. It's what I brought you up for. Now it's time to fulfill your destiny. You do love her, don't you?

PRINCE *looks at* **DAWN** *and nods.*

(Toasting) To their fairytale ending.

Fireworks go off.

Scene Ten
Eve Goes Into The Wilderness

A wasteland. **EVE** *is ragged and wet. It is raining. She is trying to construct a cover from her jacket. It collapses, spilling water all over her.*

She pulls out the necklace that the **FERTILITY WIFE** *gave her and looks at it.*

EVE Well? Aren't you supposed to do something? You said when I needed help.

A bat squeaks.

Hello?

Is anyone there?

I knew it.

You can never trust a witch.

EVE *closes her eyes.*

The necklace glows.

The space transforms into the forest.

A noise.

EVE *is on her guard.*

Who's there!

MINI *comes out. She is tiny.*

She stands.

Then **MAXI** *comes out. He is massive.*

EVE *backs away, straight into the* **FERTILITY WIFE**.

EVE *turns, terrified. She is surrounded.*

FERTILITY WIFE You should watch yourself. Little girl, all alone in the big bad woods.

EVE What do you want?

FERTILITY WIFE I thought it was you that wanted us.

The **FERTILITY WIFE** *reveals herself.*

EVE Leave me alone.

FERTILITY WIFE Very well.
Mini!
Maxi!

They make to leave.

EVE Wait!
…
Is it true you can do magic?

FERTILITY WIFE Yes.

EVE Then I need you to help me.
I need you to magic Dawn out of the palace.

FERTILITY WIFE Why?

EVE She can't see it.
She can't see how rotten that place is.
She's fallen for it all. Prince, the Queen, all of it.
I need you to get her out.

FERTILITY WIFE That I can't do.
The Queen rules there. I have only the forest.

EVE Then there's no hope.

FERTILITY WIFE Where there is beauty, there is hope.

EVE I don't understand.

FERTILITY WIFE You, Eve. You can still save Dawn. The power lies with you.

EVE Me? Ha!
Have you seen me?
I'm nothing.

FERTILITY WIFE *(putting on Pavlova's accent)* Self pity. So boring.

EVE *looks up.*

You know your mother once sat right where you are now.

EVE What?

FERTILITY WIFE Once Upon a Long Time ago. She came looking for my help.

EVE My mother was a traitor.

FERTILITY WIFE Your mother was brave.

And strong.

And she loved you... very much.

EVE That's not true.

FERTILITY WIFE Shhhhh

Close your eyes.

Listen.

I know you've been brought up to hate the forest. To hate us who live here.

But listen.

That's the wind in the trees.

And that?

That's the life of the forest.

Let it run in your veins.

As it did in your mother's.

Shhhh.

Listen.

There.

A light appears, a figure, it is the memory of **ROSE**. *We can hear* **ROSE***'s voice singing a lullaby.*

EVE Mum.

FERTILITY WIFE She can't hear you.

Beat.

She loved you, Eve.

EVE Then why did she leave me?

FERTILITY WIFE She had to. To keep you safe.

ROSE *(voice over)* Tell her I was a good person. And I'll always love her.

EVE *(going to touch the light)* Mum?

ROSE *disappears.*

What did you do?

FERTILITY WIFE Nothing.

You have such power, Eve.

The power to change things.

Even the trees still for you. See.

They're waiting for you to bring beauty back to the land.

EVE How?

FERTILITY WIFE Come.

EVE Where?

FERTILITY WIFE I am a witch, stop asking me questions and do as I say.

Scene Eleven
Cold Feet

In the castle. The night before the wedding. **DAWN** *sits. She has been crying.*

PRINCE *arrives at the door.*

PRINCE Hey.

DAWN *(wiping her face)* Hi.

PRINCE What's wrong?

DAWN Nothing.

PRINCE Really?

DAWN It feels weird. I'm getting married tomorrow and Eve's not here.

No one to tell me to shut up when I start to get nervous?

Or make me laugh before I walk down the aisle.

PRINCE Come here.

He hugs her.

You do… you do want to get married, right?

DAWN Yeah.

Of course. I mean… if that's what you want.

PRINCE Yeah. Definitely.

DAWN That's what people do, isn't it?

In fairytales.

PRINCE I don't know.

DAWN The girl always marries the prince and lives happily ever after.

PRINCE Are they like us?

DAWN Who?

PRINCE The people in fairytales?

DAWN I suppose. Though…

PRINCE What?

DAWN I don't know. I never thought about it, but the girls in stories always seem so good. They just always do the right thing. You never see Snow White worrying about whether she's got enough toilet roll in for all the dwarves. Or Cinderella getting blisters from running in that glass slipper, or pulling a muscle or something. It's like things just happen. All the mess is hidden away. They all just do the right thing all the time. I don't always do the right thing.

PRINCE Me either.

DAWN I was horrible to Eve.

PRINCE I'm sure you weren't.

DAWN I was.

> She's my friend.
>
> I shouldn't have said those things to her.
>
> I wish I could say sorry.

PRINCE Then we'll find her.

DAWN What?

PRINCE Come on. You need her.

> Who cares about the wedding. We can do it another time.

The **QUEEN** *has entered.*

QUEENIE A great many people care about the wedding…darling.

They stop.

> Now, what's all this? Getting cold feet?

DAWN No your majesty. It's just…

PRINCE Dawn wants Eve to be at the wedding.

QUEENIE Who? Oh, your little friend.

> Well, that's okay. I've already sent out someone to find her.

DAWN You have?

QUEENIE Of course. I wanted to make sure she was safe.

PRINCE I think we should go anyway mother. Just in case.

> **PRINCE** *makes to exit with* **DAWN**. *The* **QUEEN** *weaves a spell. The two stop still.*

QUEENIE Ah ah ah.

You'll be going nowhere. You hear?

DAWN AND PRINCE Yes.

QUEENIE You will get married.

DAWN AND PRINCE We will.

QUEENIE And then you will eat the apple.

And all of your beauty will be mine.

> *She flicks her wrist and the two come out of their trance.*

Now you two little lovebirds get some sleep.

Tomorrow's going to be a very special day.

Scene Twelve
The Stories Untold

The Woods.

EVE *has subtly changed.*

She looks at home in the forest.

She is being shown a giant case of old books by the **FERTILITY WIFE**.

EVE What are they?

FERTILITY WIFE Stories.

EVE *has taken a book down. She opens it. There is a sound that comes from inside. A high pitched voice. Then someone eating and letting out a burp.*

Ahhh!

Gingerlocks.

EVE What?

FERTILITY WIFE "Gingerlocks and the Three Pears." She ends up eating them all.

EVE *takes another.*

She opens it.

There is the sound of a party and a group of men chanting "Down it! Down it! Down it!"

"Not So White and the Seven Dwarves".

Another book.

Out of it comes the sound of a very high pitched "Fe Fi Fo Fum"

"Jack and the Beansprout".

They're all the stories that have been forgotten. Left untold because the people in them weren't beautiful or important enough.

We collect them. Give them a home.

EVE What's that one?

FERTILITY WIFE *(getting down a plain-looking book)* It's your story. See.

The Sleeping Beauties.

EVE Me?

FERTILITY WIFE Yes. You and Dawn.

EVE I'm in a story?

...

How does it end?

Just then there is a whistling sound and a knife hits the tree just next to **EVE**.

A scuffle and **MINI** *comes out holding* **BONE** *in an armlock.*

BONE *(screaming)* AHHHHH! Help!

MINI *whispers to the* **FERTILITY WIFE**.

FERTILITY WIFE Mini says sorry. She couldn't get to him before he'd let one off.

BONE Don't hurt me. Please.

EVE Why are you here?

BONE I can't...

The Queen will kill me.

FERTILITY WIFE This is my realm.

The Queen can't hurt you here.

BONE Are you going to turn me into a frog?

FERTILITY WIFE *(laughing)* A frog?

BONE Yeah. Or a wart or something.

EVE No, but I'll do something much, much worse with this knife if you don't tell me why you're here.

BONE To stop you ever coming back. You and your friend.

EVE Dawn? Where is she?

BONE She's in the castle.

She's getting married.

EVE What?

BONE To pretty boy… Prince.

EVE *is gutted. She drops the knife.*

Then the queen's going to kill them.

FERTILITY WIFE What?

BONE "Till death do us part."

I was supposed to find an apple, but I couldn't because of my asthma, so Poke had to do it and that meant I had to come here, which wasn't fair because I don't even like the dark, and definitely not the dark forest. And definitely not the dark forest with the witches in. I've had a horrible few days. Look! I ripped my jerkin.

EVE When do they get married?

BONE Tomorrow.

EVE *(to* **FERTILITY WIFE***)* I have to go.

I have to save her.

FERTILITY WIFE Yes.

MINI *makes a sound.*

Mini wants to go with you.

EVE Thank you.

What about him?

FERTILITY WIFE I'll have to kill him.

BONE Wait! No. I can help you. Please. I could get you into the palace. I've always hated the queen. She confiscated my stone collection.

Suddenly **EVE** *notices the forest around them. The eyes of a million animals are watching.*

EVE What's happening?

FERTILITY WIFE Something I haven't seen for a thousand years.

The forest moves. You have woken it.

They are singing your name, Eve.

They will be with you when the time comes. As will I. Wherever beauty lives.

Now go.

EVE, **MINI** *and* **BONE** *exit.*

The quickening of breath.

The night sound of owls.

Expand, let go, and see what the world will show.

***

Scene Thirteen
The Wedding Ceremony

The altar. **PRINCE** *is waiting nervously.*

The **QUEEN** *beside him.*

QUEENIE You look marvelous darling. So handsome. Everything I brought you up to be. The perfect Prince.

Suddenly **EVE** *appears, she is dressed as a priest. She is unusually tall due to* **MAXI** *and* **MINI** *hiding in her cassock. They stand awkwardly. The wedding march strikes up.* **DAWN** *appears and walks to the altar.*

DAWN Is Eve here?

EVE *almost gives herself away.*

QUEENIE No dear. She couldn't be found. I'm sure she'll turn up, maybe for the reception.

EVE Dearly beloved, we are gathered here today to witness the joining together of Princess Dawn and... him.

QUEENIE Yes yes. Get on with it.

No need for all the chit chat.

EVE Does anyone here have any reason either known or unknown or even a bit known why these two... people should not be married. For example, they might already be married to someone else or they might have committed some horrible crime or perhaps one of them is just making a huge HUGE mistake and marrying a complete IDIOT.

No?

No one?

(Pointing to someone in the audience) What about you madam? Anything? No?

Lovely bag. Where did you get that from?

QUEENIE Get on with it.

EVE Yes. Yes. And so on to the royal marriage rules.

EVE *pulls out a huge list of rules.*

QUEENIE What's that?

EVE The rules.

1. You must never ever kiss or cuddle each other without a priest's permission.

2. You must sleep in separate beds and always wear pyjamas or an equivalent. (I think that means like a onesie).

3. When saddling up a horse –

QUEENIE How many of them are there?

EVE Quite a few.

When saddling up a horse...

QUEENIE Enough.

I'll take over from here.

Do you Prince, take this... girl to be your lawfully wedded wife?

PRINCE I think so.

QUEENIE Say 'I do.'

PRINCE I do.

QUEENIE *(to* DAWN*)* And do you?

DAWN I do.

QUEENIE Then I pronounce you man and wife.

Now, as is tradition in the kingdom, the marriage can only be sealed with a bite from the apple of... love.

PRINCE What?

POKE *has brought on the apple, resting on a velvet pillow.*

QUEENIE Yes darling, it's tradition.

You both have to take a bite.

PRINCE What about the ring?

QUEENIE What?

PRINCE We haven't exchanged rings.

QUEENIE Really? You really want to do that?

Fine.

PRINCE gets out a ring. It is quite homemade looking.

PRINCE I made it myself.

I thought it might make you smile.

DAWN is charmed. The QUEEN is nearly sick.

QUEENIE There. Now.

The apple.

The apple is brought forward. PRINCE goes to reach for it.

Ah ah ah, ladies first.

DAWN looks at it.

DAWN I'm actually a bit allergic.

The QUEEN, at the end of her patience, casts a spell. DAWN, like a zombie takes the apple.

I bite this apple in love of you.

She is about to bite is when EVE jumps forward and grabs the apple.

She throws it to MAXI who catches and throws it to MINI.

QUEENIE What are you doing?

Give that back.

EVE Dawn.

It's me.

It's a trap.

The apple's poisoned.

PRINCE What?

DAWN *(Zombie like, starting to follow the apple)* I bite this apple in love of you.

PRINCE Dawn?

EVE Prince. Get her away.

It's a spell.

The queen wants to kill her.

PRINCE *struggles to hold back* **DAWN**.

QUEENIE *(tearing her wig off. Roars.)* Not just her. I will kill you *ALL*. You *STUPID, MEDDLING IMBECILES*.

She casts a spell and flattens them all.

She goes up to **EVE**.

She is now fully **CLOVE** *again. Or some kind of mix of* **CLOVE** *and the* **QUEEN**. *Her voice is low and reverberates. She is a monster.*

How dare you.

I should've dealt with you a thousand years ago.

The ugly little friend of the Princess.

I should've pulled you from your mother's belly and trodden you into the dirt.

But then again I wouldn't have the pleasure of doing this.

She electrocutes **EVE** *a bit.*

EVE *writhes in pain.*

DAWN *(waking from her trance)* Eve?

EVE *(weak)* Dawn. GO!

The **QUEEN** *is about to strike the final blow.*

DAWN Wait!

Please.

Don't.

Let her go.

QUEENIE And why would I do that?

DAWN It's me you want.

She picks up the apple, which has rolled to rest at her feet.

I'll eat the apple.

If you let her go.

QUEENIE Very well.

EVE Don't Dawn.

Please.

You have to escape.

I came to save you.

DAWN No.

I can't go without you.

We're a team. Remember?

A Day without a Night.

It just wouldn't work.

There'd be no fun in it.

Looking at the apple.

Let her go first.

QUEENIE Eat it.

I said EAT IT!

DAWN *takes a bite of the apple.*

The **QUEEN** *lets go of* **EVE** *in ecstasy.*

EVE *runs to* **DAWN**.

EVE Dawn.

Dawn.

Don't.

Please, don't leave me.

DAWN *puts out her hand for their 'special' handshake.* **EVE** *does it, sadly.*

DAWN *dies.*

QUEENIE At last.

Beauty.

Is mine.

The **QUEEN** *looks confused. It should feel... different. Just then there is the sound of voices starting to sing.*

A sound building.

It gets louder.

What's going on?

Stop it.

Stop this!

The walls of the castle are shaking now.

There is the voice of the **FERTILITY WIFE**. *Loud.*

FERTILITY WIFE "From sleep they will come from beyond the wall. Holding the key to power over all. If loved by a prince then to death one will fall. And she with true beauty will rule evermore."

QUEENIE No.

I've beaten it.

I have her beauty.

I will rule.

The **FERTILITY WIFE** *appears. She is glorious.*

FERTILITY WIFE No.

To give yourself for another.

This is true beauty.

The most powerful magic of all.

Not Dawn's or Eve's alone, but between them both.

QUEENIE No

FERTILITY WIFE And where there is beauty, there is life. You cannot stop it.

PRINCE What's happening?

The walls of the hall are shaking and cracking.

They crumble.

Through the stone things are growing.

Flowers, trees, branches.

Birds fly in and rabbits bounce through the holes in the walls.

The whole city is sprouting new life.

Through the tumbling ceiling the stars start to show.

FERTILITY WIFE The forest returns.

QUEENIE No. The city. My beautiful city.

FERTILITY WIFE Listen.

PRINCE What is it?

FERTILITY WIFE The people. Singing. They have remembered the old song that travels through us all.

QUEENIE No.
>Stop.
>You hear me?
>STOP!

*But the **QUEEN**'s power is reducing as the singing gets stronger.*

She is shrinking.

>I can't bear it.
>I can't bear it.
>Stop the music please.
>Stop it.

FERTILITY WIFE You will shrink, you will wither.
>You will leave this place of beauty.
>I cast you out.
>GO!

*The **QUEEN** shrivels till she is just a pile of clothes, then screams off into the night, a vapour.*

PRINCE *goes over to* **EVE** *who has tears on her face.*

PRINCE She loved you.

EVE I know.

PRINCE I loved her too.

> **EVE** *nods and lets herself cry.*
>
> *She kisses* **DAWN** *on the lips, then hugs her hard.*
>
> *The hug is so strong that the piece of apple* **DAWN** *has eaten shoots from her mouth.*
>
> **DAWN** *wakes up.*

DAWN Why are you all crying?

EVE Dawn.

DAWN What happened?

EVE You died.

DAWN Did I?
> That's funny.
> You'd think it'd be a bit more dramatic.

EVE You're alive.
> You're alive.

> **EVE** *hugs* **DAWN**.

DAWN Well, I couldn't leave you to all the action, could I? Besides I knew you'd save me. No matter what. That's what friends are for.

FERTILITY WIFE And the forest will grow once more.

EVE Now that Clove is dead.

FERTILITY WIFE Not dead.
> He will always be there, somewhere, just as I will.
>
> There will always be two forces in the world, It is your job to achieve balance in the kingdom.
>
> You must be wise.
>
> And just.

The two of you.

Dawn and Eve.

EVE Night…

DAWN And Day.

PRINCE And me.

Don't forget me. "Afternoon!"

FERTILITY WIFE Farewell.

EVE Wait!

Where are you going?

I haven't finished learning the ways of the forest. The stories.

FERTILITY WIFE Then come to me, whenever you need to. But for now your place is here.

There are other things you must learn.

Farewell Eve and Dawn

Farewell my sleeping beauties.

The **FERTILITY WIFE** *flies away.*

EVE Ha!

DAWN What?

EVE I've just realised something.

DAWN What?

EVE You're married.

DAWN No I'm not.

EVE You are.

You went through with it. The ceremony.

DAWN But I didn't know what I was doing.

EVE That's what everyone says.

The day after.

PRINCE It's okay.

I'm fairly sure the marriage wasn't strictly legal.

DAWN It's not that I wouldn't marry you.

Just, maybe not for a bit eh?

PRINCE Yeah.

I've got to play the field anyway.

DAWN What?

PRINCE That's what princes do. They play around, then they marry someone boring.

DAWN Boring!

PRINCE Their cousin, normally.

EVE *goes to leave.*

Where are you going?

EVE Well, if you two are going to be all lovey dovey I'm going to check out the palace. See what secrets Queenie had locked away.

DAWN We'll come with you.

EVE Okay, but only if you keep your hands off each other and stop making all those… love eyes.

DAWN Love eyes?

EVE *(doing an impression in a baby voice)* "Oooooh Princey what nice arms you have."

DAWN Shut up!

EVE It's true. It's gross. It's like being with a pair of swans.

DAWN Swans?

EVE Yeah. Like being with two of the most boring swans in the world. All beautiful and "ooooh, look at my neck. Isn't it fine?" "Oh yes, your neck is fine. Isn't my neck fine?" "Oh, your neck is lovely. I'd like to touch it. Oh we're the most beautiful swans in the world. Let's mate for life." EUGH!

PRINCE Oi!

DAWN And what about you?

EVE Me? I'm hanging out with all the weird birds. Who some of them aren't even birds, they're just water voles who think they're birds. But that's fine. And we've all got wonky feathers. Or dirty beaks. And we can't be bothered to swim everywhere. We're having our own party. In the reeds. We look at you swans and we pity you.

DAWN Pity?

EVE Yeah. Because you don't even know we're there. You just keep looking at your own reflection and thinking that's it. We're the swans.

Well, I'm here to tell you the swans are over. The swans have had their day.

The weird birds are out and we're taking over the pond.

And there's nothing you can do to stop it.

Ha!

Dawn goes to grab **EVE**. *She's too quick. They all run off.*

***

Epilogue

FERTILITY WIFE And so they lived happily ever after. Or so the story goes.

The **FERTILITY WIFE** *sings a final ending.*

www.ingramcontent.com/pod-product-compliance
Ingram Content Group UK Ltd.
Pitfield, Milton Keynes, MK11 3LW, UK
UKHW021831140426
5217IPUK00021B/1381